Mammals of
Great Smoky Mountains

NATIONAL PARK

The McDonald & Woodward Publishing Company
P. O. Box 10308, Blacksburg, Virginia 24062-0308

Mammals of Great Smoky Mountains National Park

All rights reserved. First printing, January 1995.
Printed in Hong Kong by Sing Cheong Printing Company, Ltd.

01 00 99 98 97 96 95   10 9 8 7 6 5 4 3 2 1

Library of Congress Cataloging-in-Publication Data

Linzey, Donald W.
    Mammals of Great Smoky Mountains National Park / by Donald
W. Linzey.
      p.   cm.
    Includes bibliographical references (p.   ) and index.
    ISBN 0-939923-48-3 (paper) : $14.95
    1. Mammals — Great Smoky Mountains National Park (N.C. and
Tenn.) 2. Great Smoky Mountains National Park (N.C. and Tenn.)
I. Title.
QL719.N8L55   1995
599.09768'89 — dc20   94-39382
                                                        CIP

To Mom and Dad

*who introduced me
to the Smokies*

Contents

Preface   ix

Introduction   1

Mammals of the Park   7

Mammals of Surrounding Areas   101

Glossary   105

Literature Cited   109

Appendix I. Checklist of Mammals   117

Appendix II. Localities Referred to in Text   121

Appendix III. Photographers Credits   133

Index   135

Preface

Mammals of Great Smoky Mountains National Park was originally published in 1971 by The University of Tennessee Press. It was designed and written for the park visitor who wished to become acquainted with the distribution and habits of the various types of mammals in the Great Smokies. A total of 67 mammals were listed and discussed, including six extirpated forms. The book was based on a comprehensive technical paper (Linzey and Linzey, 1968) that included all available information on the park's mammals. A similar comprehensive technical paper dealing with the mammals of the Great Smokies today is currently in preparation (Linzey, in press).

During the ensuing 23 years, significant changes occurred in the mammalian fauna of the park. This revision contains reviews of 70 mammals of which only four are extirpated. Two species (hoary bat and coyote) new to the park have been recorded, while another two species (river otter and red wolf) have been successfully reintroduced. The mountain lion, formerly considered to be extirpated, may be present in low numbers in the park. Many new locality and elevation records, as well as natural history information, have been recorded for species within the park. The inclusion of the Foothills Parkway in the park's jurisdiction has added a cave (Myhr Cave) and additional areas of early successional habitat. Several species of mammals now considered rare in the park have been found in suitable habitat along the parkway. Numerous taxonomic revisions have also occurred since 1971.

The author is deeply indebted to Arthur Stupka, former park biologist, for his faith in my wife and myself, for his many suggestions during the course of our research, and for his aid in preparing the 1971 manuscript. If it were not for his keen interest in the fauna of the Smokies, much of the information reported here would never have been recorded. In addition, I wish to thank National Park Service personnel Gene Cox, Don DeFoe, Kim DeLozier, Annette Evans, Keith Langdon, and Kitty Manscill for their help in obtaining data for this revision. I also wish to thank the many curators of museums throughout the United States for searching their collections and for making specimens and data available.

Introduction

Visitors to Great Smoky Mountains National Park are likely to see a variety of wildlife species during their visit. A wide variety of animals — salamanders, turtles, lizards, snakes, birds, and mammals — inhabit the park. Some of them are abundant and readily seen, whereas others are rarely noticed by the casual observer.

This book focuses on the park's mammals. Mammals are the fur-bearing animals that nurse their young. Mammals that occur in the park range in size from the pygmy shrew that weighs approximately 1/12 ounce (2.5 grams) and reaches a total length of 3 to 3 1/2 inches (75 to 87 millimeters) to the black bear which normally weighs 100 to 300 pounds (45 to 135 kilograms) but which may occasionally weigh over 500 pounds (225 kilograms). Woodchucks feeding along the side of the road, white-tailed deer grazing in Cades Cove, and chipmunks seen in the campgrounds and picnic areas are just a few of the 70 different species of mammals that have been recorded from the area now included in the park. Most are current inhabitants, although some such as the bison, elk, and fisher disappeared long before the establishment of the national park.

Twenty-seven of the 66 varieties of mammals (41 percent) currently inhabiting the park are gnawing animals and are classified as rodents. This group includes the woodchucks, chipmunks, squirrels, beavers, mice, and rats. In addition, there are eight species of shrews, three moles, ten bats, two rabbits, two foxes, the red wolf, the coyote, the raccoon, the black bear, the opossum, the long-tailed weasel, the mink, the otter, two skunks, two cats, the white-tailed deer, and the wild hog.

Some mammals, such as the black bear and white-tailed deer, are large and readily visible. Many others, however, such as the shrews, moles, and mice are small, secretive, and rarely seen by visitors. In addition, some mammals are seen only during the warmer months because they either become inactive and hibernate during the winter or, in the case of some bats, migrate to warmer regions. The hibernating species include the woodchuck, chipmunk, some native mice, and some bats. These forms pass the colder, unfavorable season by becoming dormant; some, such as the jumping mice, remain dormant for as long as five to six months.

Different mammals occur in different parts of the park. Certain kinds are only found at low elevations such as Cades Cove, Elkmont, Sugarlands, Cosby, Smokemont, and Deep Creek, whereas others will be found primarily in the high elevation spruce-fir forests in areas such as Newfound Gap, Mount LeConte, and Clingmans Dome.

The present distribution of mammal species in the park is directly related to the types of habitats available, the occurrence and extent of each habitat type being a result of various climatic and historical factors. Local climatic conditions vary widely in an area that ranges from 857 feet (260 meters) along Abrams Creek to 6,643 feet (2,025 meters) on the summit of Clingmans Dome. As elevation increases, precipitation increases but temperatures decrease. Annual precipitation ranges from about 55 inches (1,397 millimeters) near Gatlinburg to about 85 inches (2,159 millimeters) on Clingmans Dome. Average temperatures decrease 2.23 degrees F for every 1,000-foot (305 meters) increase in elevation. Thus, sea-level climates most nearly equivalent to those of high elevations in the Smokies may occur about 1,000 miles (1,600 killometers) to the northeast, in northeastern Maine (Shanks, 1954). The difference in climatic conditions at higher elevations results in substantially different vegetation communities which, in turn, quite often support populations of animals that could not survive under conditions at lower elevations. This variation in climate and vegetation helps explain why the ranges of a number of northern species of mammals extend down the Appalachian Mountain chain and reach or approach their southern limit in the park area. Some shrews and the red squirrel, northern flying squirrel, and rock vole require the conditions at higher elevations. Others, such as the least shrew, fox squirrel, beaver, harvest mouse, golden mouse, muskrat, and spotted skunk are normally found below approximately 4,000 feet (1,220 meters) elevation.

Present climatic conditions alone, however, cannot totally explain the geographic distribution of many species of mammals. During the Pleistocene epoch of the last Ice Age, which began approximately one million years ago, most of Canada and much of the northern part of the United States were periodically covered by extensive ice sheets. During periods when glaciers were forming, the ranges of many species of plants and animals were slowly displaced southward. Since the glacial advances halted far north of the Smokies, the Southern Appalachians and adjacent regions became refuges for species that previously had been typical of more northern areas. As the region warmed and the glaciers retreated, the ranges of many of these forms then expanded northward where environments were again hospitable. Since climatic conditions at high elevations in the southern mountains are similar to those at lower elevations in northern areas, some populations of northern species, such as the water shrew, northern flying squirrel, red squirrel, and rock vole have remained far south of their primary range and persisted in the Great Smokies to the present day. These more or less isolated populations are known as disjunct populations.

Changing Mammal Populations

Prior to the mid-1700s, the area now composing the Great Smoky Mountains National Park was largely uninhabited, although the Cherokee Indians lived nearby in such communities as Cherokee and along the Little Tennessee River. The Cherokees probably hunted to some extent, but their effect on mammal populations was probably minimal. Significant ecological changes began when early settlers of European extraction started arriving in greater numbers during the mid- to late 1700s. Especially at lower elevations, the diversity of mammal habitats was greatly increased by clearing land for homesteads and cultivation. This marked the beginning of a trend that was not to be reversed until acquisition of land for the park commenced in the 1920s. Human habitation increased throughout the nineteenth century, and the changes accelerated steadily. This trend reached a peak in the early 1900s when the activities of logging companies drastically altered huge tracts of land in a very short time. It has been estimated that, by the time the park was dedicated in 1940, more than two-thirds of the land had been cut over.

The settlement of the mountains undoubtedly had a substantial effect on mammal populations. Although there is little documented evidence of these effects, our present knowledge of the ecology of the various species indicates the changes that must have occurred. Settlement of the park area had a direct effect on some animals; for example, the gray wolf, river otter, mountain lion, and white-tailed deer were victims of hunting and trapping. On the other hand, populations of several game or fur species, such as black bears, opossums, squirrels, raccoons, and foxes, apparently withstood these pressures.

Some species of mammals were affected in a more indirect fashion. As land at lower elevations was cleared and cut over, a different type of mammal habitat was created. Species that inhabit open areas or forest edges were able to extend their ranges into these new habitats. The white-tailed deer, characteristically an animal of the forest edge, was one species that benefited from land-clearing operations. Deer were probably less common in the Great Smokies prior to the time the land was cleared and cut over, but they apparently became fairly abundant during the 1800s. Land cleared for cultivation and subsequently abandoned was also particularly hospitable for certain species of small mammals, such as the least shrew, eastern harvest mouse, rice rat, and hispid cotton rat.

The decline of the American chestnut was another factor that seriously affected the populations of many species of mammals. The chestnut blight fungus is thought to have arrived in the area in the mid-1920s. It has been estimated that, by 1938, 85 percent of the chestnut trees in the park had been killed or affected by the blight. Mammals such as squirrels and bears that had depended on chestnut mast for their food supply were gradually forced to depend on acorns instead. Currently, populations of flowering dogwood, Fraser fir, beech, and butternut are declining because of a variety of factors including acid rain, insects, and rooting by hogs. The loss of these important species of trees will affect many species of mammals.

The protection afforded by the park has allowed some mammal species to increase to considerable numbers, while others have declined as a result of the decrease in human influence. Due to hunting and other factors, the white-tailed deer population in the area had declined almost to the point of extirpation just prior to the establishment of the park. Since coming under park protection, however, deer have been increasing and populations are now well established. Growth of oak forests in areas where the American chestnut has disappeared undoubtedly had a beneficial effect on mast-eating animals, such as squirrels and bears. Many forest-dwelling species of small mammals have also profited by the extension of their habitats due to reforestation. A study of the vegetation patterns along a section of the park border near Cosby together with the effects of park border placement on the distribution and movements of small mammals was reported by Ambrose (1986). Habitat differences along some border sites appeared to influence the home range orientation of the white-footed mouse.

The first extensive survey of mammals in the park was undertaken between 1931 and 1933 and reported in the scientific paper entitled *Mammals of the Great Smoky Mountains* (Komarek and Komarek, 1938). From that time until 1968, there were several published notes regarding particular species of park mammals as well as unpublished reports by numerous individuals that were deposited in the park files.

Arthur Stupka, former chief naturalist and park biologist for the Great Smoky Mountains National Park kept a journal for 28 years (1935 to 1962). This journal included not only personal observations but also substantiated reports of others. Copies of the journal reside in the park archives and the library of the United States Department of the Interior.

The author began working in the park in June, 1963. His research resulted in several publications (see Literature Cited), among them a comprehensive paper including all available information on mammals of the park (Linzey and Linzey, 1968) and a book for the park visitor who wished to become acquainted with the distribution and habits of the various types of mammals that occurred in the park (Linzey and Linzey, 1971). Portions of the preceding overview of changes in the numbers and distribution of mammals in the park were taken from Linzey and Linzey (1971).

Since the mid-1970s, Dr. Michael Pelton of the University of Tennessee has contributed a great deal to our knowledge of certain mammals through his research and that of his graduate students. Other researchers, including Dr. W. David Webster, Dr. Peter Weigl, and Dr. Michael Harvey have also contributed valuable data. The establishment of the Twin Creeks Natural Resource Center within the park in the early 1970s by the National Park Service has served to coordinate research efforts by visiting investigators.

Mammal Accounts _____

In order to assist the visitor in identifying mammals observed in the park, a numerical code is provided at the beginning of each account. This code provides a quick reference to the elevations from which the species has been recorded within the park. The code is as follows:

Below 1,999 feet	-	1
2,000 to 2,999 feet	-	2
3,000 to 3,999 feet	-	3
4,000 to 4,999 feet	-	4
5,000 to 5,999 feet	-	5
Over 6,000 feet	-	6

A hiker on the Appalachian Trail, for example, need only refer to mammals with a 4, 5, or 6 designation, whereas a camper in Cades Cove or Elkmont would generally need only to check those with a 1 or 2 to identify an animal seen in that area.

Mammals are mobile and sometimes explore areas outside their normal range. Thus, on rare occasions the possibility exists that an individual mammal may be found at either a higher or lower elevation than previously recorded in the park.

In the following species accounts, measurements are given in English units — inches (in), ounces (oz), and pounds (lbs) followed by their metric equivalents — millimeters (mm), grams (g), and kilograms (kg). Elevations for specific locality records are given in feet. A list of all localities referred to in the text together with their elevation(s) in both English and metric units is given in Appendix II.

Mammals of the Park

OPOSSUMS
Family Didelphidae

Opossums belong to a group of mammals commonly known as marsupials. Most marsupials are found in Australia and South America and include the kangaroos, wallabies, koala bears, wombats, and others. The opossum is the only marsupial in North America.

Female opossums possess an external abdominal pouch (marsupium) which encloses the teats and serves as a pocket in which the young are carried following their birth. Uterine development is brief in these mammals, and the young are born at a very incomplete stage of development. Opossums also exhibit a number of internal modifications that serve to differentiate them from other mammals.

Opossums are primarily nocturnal, and most are either arboreal or terrestrial. The hind foot possesses four claw-bearing toes and a thumblike, clawless, opposable "big toe." The snout is long and pointed, and the tail is prehensile and used for grasping.

VIRGINIA OPOSSUM
Didelphis virginiana

Tennessee - North Carolina — 1, 2, 3, 4, 5, 6

Total Length : 24 – 35 in (600 – 875 mm)
Tail : 11 – 14 in (275 – 350 mm)
Weight : 3 – 6 lbs (1.3 – 4.5 kg)

The Virginia opossum is a medium-sized mammal with long, rather coarse, grayish-white fur. The muzzle is sharp and slender; the large ears are thin, leathery, and naked; and the prehensile tail is long, scaly, and sparsely haired. The nose is pink and

7

the eyes are black. The Virginia opossum possesses 50 teeth - more than any other mammal in the park.

The Virginia opossum prefers low, damp, wooded areas along streams and swamps. Farming areas having hedgerows and small, wooded streams are preferred over densely forested upland areas.

Virginia opossums are found throughout most of the park and along the Foothills Parkway, although they decrease in abundance at the higher elevations. The highest elevation at which an individual has been observed is 6,200 feet on Noland Divide. Opossums are about throughout the year but may hole up during cold periods.

The Virginia opossum is omnivorous, eating a wide variety of foods but preferring animal matter during all seasons. It is often called a scavenger because of its habits of feeding on garbage and carrion. In the park, foods include blackberries, pokeberries, wild grapes, persimmons, millipedes, snakes, wood frogs, toads, and screech owls (Linzey and Linzey, 1971).

The reproductive season in the park extends from late winter to early summer. As many as 18 young may be born after a gestation of only 12 1/2 days, the shortest gestation of any American mammal. Usually about seven survive the period of pouch life which lasts approximately two months following their birth. The young remain near the mother for three or four weeks after leaving the pouch. During this time, they often travel on the back of the female.

These mammals are probably best known for their death-feigning act known as "playing 'possum." This action, which apparently has survival value, has been compared to fainting or temporary paralysis. It appears to be a reaction controlled by the nervous system and probably is not deliberate or willful.

SHREWS

Family Soricidae

This family includes the smallest mammals. Eight species of shrews occur within the Great Smoky Mountains National Park. They range in size from the pygmy shrew, weighing approximately 1/12 oz (2.5 g), to the big short-tailed shrew which weighs between 1/2 and 3/4 oz (14 to 21 g).

Shrews possess long tapering snouts, tiny eyes that are probably capable of only limited vision, and ears that are barely visible. Hearing and smell are acute. The tips of the incisor teeth are dark chestnut in color. Shrews somewhat resemble moles, but are generally smaller and have feet that are all the same size.

Shrews are active during all seasons. They are active throughout most of the day, with scattered short periods of rest. Most are terrestrial, although some are semi-aquatic.

Shrews feed primarily upon insects, spiders, worms, and other invertebrates (Linzey and Linzey, 1973). Predators include snakes, owls, hawks, and carnivorous mammals including opossums, foxes, bobcats, weasels, and skunks.

Members of this family possess scent glands along the sides of their bodies. This odor may function as a pheromone to attract members of the same species. It may also be used to mark territories.

Shrews are extremely nervous. When frightened, their heart may beat 1,200 times per minute, and they often die of fright from loud noises, even from thunder. The average breathing rate of captive short-tailed shrews at rest is about 168 breaths per minute, while the average heart rate is about 750 beats per minute.

Little is known about the breeding habits of most shrews. Most breed from spring to late summer with females producing several litters of three to six young each. Few wild shrews live longer than about 18 months.

Most shrews are difficult to identify to the species level, and identification is best left to an expert.

MASKED SHREW
Sorex cinereus

Tennessee - North Carolina — 2, 3, 4, 5, 6

Total Length : 3 1/2 – 4 in (85 – 100 mm)
Tail : 1 1/4 – 1 1/2 in (30 – 40 mm)
Weight : 1/10 – 1/4 oz (3 – 7 g)

The masked shrew ranges from dark brown to brownish-gray on the back with pale gray underparts. The tail is relatively long and is indistinctly bicolored.

Masked shrews are most commonly found among rocks and logs in moist woods. In the park, they have frequently been taken above 3,000 feet in both deciduous and evergreen forests, although several have been taken at Smokemont (2,200 feet) and along Buck Prong (2,500 feet). Thirteen individuals were taken along the Foothills Parkway between Cove Creek and Caney Creek at elevations ranging from 1,430 to 2,400 feet (Harvey, 1991). Other localities include Greenbrier, Dry Sluice Gap, Rocky Spring Gap, Buck Fork (4,500 feet), Flat Creek (4,900 feet), Walker Prong, Indian Gap (5,200 feet), between Forney Ridge and Andrews Bald (6,000 feet), Mount Kephart (5,600 to 6,200 feet), Mount Guyot, Mount Collins (6,100 feet), Old Black Mountain (6,300 feet), and Clingmans Dome (6,642 feet). The Great Smoky Mountains National Park is near the southern limit of the range of this shrew.

Eight masked shrews were found in the stomach of a bobcat taken on the Newfound Gap Road in Tennessee at an elevation of 3,700 feet.

SOUTHEASTERN SHREW
Sorex longirostris

Tennessee — 1

Total Length : 3 – 41/4 in (72 – 108 mm)
Tail : 1 – 1 3/4 in (25 – 40 mm)
Weight : 1/10 – 1/5 oz (3 – 6 g)

The southeastern shrew is reddish-brown above and grayish below. The long tail is indistinctly bicolored. It is slightly smaller and more reddish than the masked shrew.

This species occurs in a variety of habitats from fields to forests. Habitat in early stages of succession and disturbed habitat such as cultivated fields and abandoned fields with dense ground cover of honeysuckle, grasses, sedges, and herbs seem to be favored.

Only three southeastern shrews have been recorded in the park. They were taken in Greenbrier in 1934 and 1938 and near park headquarters in 1950. However, fifteen individuals were taken along the Foothills Parkway between Cove Creek and Maples Ranch at elevations ranging from 1,430 to 2,400 feet (Harvey, 1991).

Although this shrew may be more abundant than numbers indicate, it has undoubtedly been affected by the gradual disappearance of early successional habitat within the park boundaries.

SMOKEY SHREW
Sorex fumeus

Tennessee - North Carolina — 1, 2, 3, 4, 5, 6,

Total Length : 4 – 5 in (100 – 125 mm)
Tail : 1 1/2 – 2 in (37 – 50 mm)
Weight : 1/10 – 1/5 oz (3 – 6 g)

During the summer, the smokey shrew is a medium-sized, uniformly dull brown shrew. Its uniform coloration helps to distinguish it from the masked shrew which is dark brown or brownish-gray above with paler gray or silvery underparts. During the winter, the pelage of the smokey shrew is usually a uniform gray. The bicolored tail is brownish above and yellowish below.

These shrews are most abundant in cool, damp woodlands with a deep layer of leaf mold on the ground. Streamsides, both in evergreen and deciduous forests, are a favored habitat. This species is near the southern limit of its range in the Great Smoky Mountains National Park where it is found at all elevations.

WATER SHREW
Sorex palustris

Tennessee - North Carolina — 1, 2, 3, 4,

Total Length : 5 1/2 – 6 1/2 in (135 – 165 mm)
Tail : 2 1/2 – 3 in (60 – 75 mm)
Weight : 1/3 – 1/2 oz (9 – 14 g)

The water shrew is the largest shrew in the park. It is blackish-gray dorsally and pale to dark gray below. The feet are whitish, and the tail is indistinctly bicolored. A conspicuous fringe of stiff hairs is present along the sides of the feet and toes. The third and fourth hind toes are joined for slightly more than half of their length by a thin web.

The more or less aquatic water shrew lives beneath the overhanging banks and in rock crevices along the edges of swiftly flowing mountain streams. Rhododendron and yellow birch are usually the dominant vegetation in these areas.

This shrew readily takes to the water. The large, hair-fringed feet and toes together with the dense fur make the water shrew well adapted for swimming. It can swim, dive, float, run along the bottom of a stream, and has even been observed running upon the surface of the water for some distance. These shrews are primarily nocturnal and are active during all seasons. They feed primarily on small aquatic organisms that they capture while swimming.

Water shrews were first discovered in the park in 1950 along the West Prong of the Little Pigeon River (Conaway and Pfitzer, 1952). They have since been found living along Walker Prong and other tributaries of the Little Pigeon River from 3,700 feet to 4,700 feet elevation. They have also been taken by the author in 1980 along a tributary of the Middle Prong of the Little Pigeon River in Greenbrier at an elevation of between 1,925 and 2,000 feet, the lowest elevation ever recorded for this species in the Appalachian Mountains (Linzey, 1984). The only North Carolina record of this shrew from the park was obtained by the author from Beech Flats Prong (4,000 feet) in Swain County in 1980 (Linzey, 1984). This represents the only record for the Oconaluftee watershed.

LONG-TAILED SHREW
Sorex dispar

Tennessee - North Carolina — 3, 4, 5, 6

Total Length : 4 1/2 – 5 1/4 in (110 – 132 mm)
Tail : 2 – 2 3/8 in (50 – 59 mm)
Weight : 1/10 – 1/4 oz (4 – 8 g)

The long-tailed shrew is a medium-sized shrew with slate-gray pelage. The underparts may be slightly paler than the back. The long, thick, sparsely haired tail is nearly uniform in color, being blackish above and only slightly paler below. The feet are whitish.

Long-tailed shrews are found primarily at the higher elevations in the park, although several have been recorded in Greenbrier. Localities include Fort Harry Cliffs (3,200 feet), along the West Prong of the Little Pigeon River (3,700 to 4,700 feet), along Newfound Gap Road in North Carolina (4,400 feet), and on Clingmans Dome (6,400 to 6,642 feet).

These shrews live in both deciduous and coniferous forests. Preferred habitat includes talus slopes and rock slides. They also inhabit the subterranean tunnels that occur in the rocky crevices between boulders and sometimes have been taken beneath moss-covered logs in damp coniferous forests. Individuals in the park have been recorded feeding on beetles and spiders.

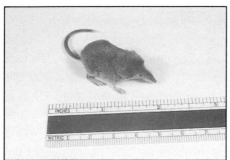

PYGMY SHREW
Sorex hoyi

North Carolina — 5

Total Length : 2 3/4 – 3 3/8 in (70 – 85 mm)
Tail : 1 – 1 1/4 in (25 – 30 mm)
Weight : 1/10 – 1/7 oz (2 – 4 g)

The pygmy shrew is one of the rarest shrews in the park. It was not until 1968 that a previously unreported specimen was discovered in the collections of the University of Illinois Museum of Natural History (Hoffmeister, 1968). It had been taken on September 6, 1941, at Newfound Gap, Swain County, North Carolina. No other individuals were recorded until 1991 when six shrews were taken along the Foothills Parkway at Cove Creek (1,430 feet), King Hollow Branch (1,700 to 1,800 feet), and Caney Creek (1,800 to 2,100 feet) (Harvey, 1991).

The pygmy shrew is the smallest mammal in North America and among the smallest in the world by weight. Adults weigh approximately the same as a dime. The fur is grayish-brown above and grayish below. The tail is indistinctly bicolored.

The habitat of pygmy shrews ranges from old fields to hardwood and coniferous forests. They have been taken under decaying logs as well as in deep leaf litter.

SHORT-TAILED SHREW
Blarina brevicauda

Tennessee - North Carolina — 1, 2, 3, 4, 5, 6

Total Length : 3 3/4 – 4 1/4 in (95 – 108 mm)
Tail: 3/4 – 1 1/4 in (18 – 30 mm)
Weight: 1/2 – 1 oz (14 – 28 g)

In overall length, the short-tailed shrew is the second largest of the eight species of shrews found in the park. By weight, however, it is the heaviest. The short, dense, velvety fur is uniformly slate-gray with slightly paler underparts. The short tail is well-haired. The eyes are minute, and the ears are so small that they are hidden in the fur.

In the park, the short-tailed shrew can be found in almost all kinds of habitats at all elevations. Moist woodland bordering swamps and streams with some leaf litter and low herbaceous vegetation seems to be preferred.

These shrews are active mainly at night. They have poor eyesight but highly developed senses of smell and touch. Tactile stimuli are received via the vibrissae and snout. They use echolocation for exploring their environment.

These shrews make shallow runways beneath the surface litter. They also use the burrows and runways of other animals. Nests of dry leaves and grasses are constructed beneath logs, stumps, and rocks. Individuals generally are solitary except during the mating season.

The short-tailed shrew is the only poisonous mammal in North America. The poison is produced by the submaxillary salivary gland and is present in the saliva. It acts as a slow poison and immobilizes insects and other prey. Immobilized insects remain alive for three to five days and provide a source of fresh non-decomposing food. Mice and rabbits injected with a submaxillary gland secretion exhibited a local reaction, lowering of the blood pressure, slowing of the heart, and inhibition of respiration (Pearson, 1942). Few records are available concerning the effect of this poison on man, although the bite may cause considerable discomfort and has been known to produce local swelling (Maynard, 1889; Krosch, 1973).

These shrews have a particularly strong musky odor. For this reason, some predators such as foxes and bobcats may kill these shrews but not eat them. Freshly killed short-tailed shrews are frequently found along park trails, particularly at the higher elevations. Some predators do consume them, however. In the park, known predators include copperheads, black rat snakes, barred owls, and spotted skunks.

LEAST SHREW
Cryptotis parva

Tennessee — 1, 2

Total Length : 2 3/4 – 3 1/4 in (70 – 80 mm)
Tail : 1/2 – 3/4 in (12 – 19 mm)
Weight : 1/10 – 1/5 oz (3 – 6 g)

The least shrew is the smaller of the two short-tailed shrews that occur in the park and is the shortest of all of the park's mammals. The upperparts are dark grayish-brown, while the underparts are somewhat paler.

This shrew, unlike most species, prefers dry, open, grassy fields. These types of habitats have been decreasing in the park as cultivated areas yield to the regrowth of forest. Localities from which this species has been recorded in the park include the Foothills Parkway at Cove Creek (1,430 feet), Fighting Creek (1,442 feet), Cades Cove, Cosby, Gatlinburg, Park Headquarters area (1,500 feet), Elkmont, Greenbrier Cove (1,800 feet), and Fish Camp Prong (2,730 feet).

These shrews are primarily nocturnal and are active at all seasons. Unlike most shrews, this species is gregarious. Nests containing as many as 31 individuals have been reported elsewhere in its range. Approximately 25 least shrews were found in a leaf nest beneath a log in Virginia (Jackson, 1961). This behavior may serve as a heat conservation measure.

MOLES

Family Talpidae

Moles are highly specialized for subterranean life. Their soft, silky, dense fur lies equally well when brushed either forward or backward, an adaptation to facilitate movement in either direction in the underground burrow. The short front limbs possess feet that are greatly enlarged for digging. The forefeet are at least as broad as they are long, and the palms face outward. The claws on the forefeet are broad and flat, while those of the hind feet are relatively short and weak. The tiny, degenerate eyes are concealed in the fur and are covered by fused eyelids. External ears are absent.

Moles may be active at any hour and during all seasons. They feed primarily on earthworms and other invertebrates.

Three kinds of moles occur within the Great Smoky Mountains National Park.

EASTERN MOLE
Scalopus aquaticus

Tennessee - North Carolina — 1, 2

Total Length : 5 1/2 – 8 in (135 – 200 mm)
Tail : 3/4 – 1 1/2 in (22 – 40 mm)
Weight : 3 1/2 – 5 oz (100 – 140 g)

The grayish-brown fur of the eastern mole is frequently stained brownish or yellowish by secretions of oil glands on the head, chin, wrist, and belly. The face, feet, and tail are whitish or pinkish. The tail is short and sparsely haired. The nostrils open upward at the end of the long, pointed, and naked nose.

Eastern moles prefer moist, sandy, or loamy soil. They occur in meadows, gardens, cultivated fields, river bottoms, mountain slopes, and forests. They have only been recorded from six areas within the park. These include Cataloochee, Greenbrier, Cades Cove, Metcalf Bottoms, Cosby, and Oconaluftee. Elevations range from 1,750 feet (Cades Cove) to 2,700 feet (Cosby). Many individuals have been recorded from the field adjoining the Oconaluftee Visitor Center (2,100 feet).

The temporary, or feeding, tunnels constructed just beneath the surface of the ground produce low ridges and mounds of earth on the ground surface. These are the most visible indication of the mole's presence. Lower level tunnels contain the mole's living quarters and nest sites. These tunnels may be as much as 24 inches (60 cm) beneath the surface.

An eastern mole was found in the stomach of a copperhead in the Cataloochee area.

HAIRY-TAILED MOLE
Parascalops breweri

Tennessee - North Carolina — 1, 2, 3, 4, 5, 6

Total Length : 5 1/2 – 7 in (135 – 175 mm)
Tail : 1 – 1 1/2 in (25 – 35 mm)
Weight : 1 1/2 – 2 1/4 oz (40 – 65 g)

The robust hairy-tailed mole has shiny, black fur and a short, hairy tail. It is the smallest of the park's moles. The eyes are minute, external ears are absent, and the nostrils are lateral and crescent-shaped.

The hairy-tailed mole prefers well-drained areas with sandy loam soil and a good cover of vegetation. In the park, these moles have been found at elevations ranging from 1,480 feet (park headquarters) to 6,400 feet (Clingmans Dome). Other localities include The Sinks (1,565 feet), Cades Cove (1,750 feet), Sugarlands (2,000 feet), Greenbrier (2,000 feet), Elkmont (2,200 to 2,500 feet), Tremont (2,400 feet), Cosby (2,600 feet), Rainbow Falls Trail (3,000 feet), Chapman Prong (3,200 feet), Bote Mountain road (3,600 feet), Alum Cave Trail (4,300 feet; 5,800 feet), Gregory Bald (4,900 feet), Miry Ridge Trail (5,000 feet), Spence Field (5,000 feet), Newfound Gap (5,050 feet), Blanket Mountain, Mount Kephart (5,200 feet), Mount Collins (5,500; 5,800 feet), and Mount Buckley (6,250 feet).

Both surface tunnels and deep tunnels are constructed. These moles are active at all hours and during all seasons. During the colder months, most activity is usually confined to the deeper tunnels.

STAR-NOSED MOLE
Condylura cristata

Tennessee - North Carolina — 1, 2, 3, 4, 5

Total Length : 6 1/2 – 8 1/2 in (160 – 210 mm)
Tail : 2 1/2 – 3 1/2 in (60 – 90 mm)
Weight : 1 – 2 1/2 oz (30 – 75 g)

The star-nosed mole is the rarest of the three moles in the park. The fur ranges from blackish-brown to black. The long, hairy tail is constricted near the base. The most unique feature consists of 22 fleshy rays arising from the nose. These highly sensitive tactile processes are used for detecting potential food items. They are richly supplied with nerves and blood vessels. Recent studies suggest that the rays may be correlated with the use of electroreception to detect prey (Gould et al., 1993). Sight and smell are poorly developed.

Star-nosed moles are semi-aquatic and prefer low, wet areas such as wet meadows, marshes, and low wet ground near streams. They have been found from 1,600 feet (Little River Road) to 5,500 feet elevation (Charlies Bunion) in the park. Other localities include Deep Creek (2,200 feet), Smokemont, Kephart Prong Hatchery (2,800 feet), Rainfall Falls Trail (3,000 feet), Miry Ridge Trail (4,900 feet), and along the Appalachian Trail between Newfound Gap and Indian Gap (5,300 feet).

These moles are excellent swimmers, and some of their burrows often have underwater openings. They are active both day and night during all seasons. Food consists primarily of aquatic and terrestrial worms and aquatic insects. Corn snakes and domestic cats are the only predators recorded within the park.

BATS
Family Vespertilionidae

Bats are unique among mammals because their forelimbs are specialized for true flight. Flight membranes, which are actually extensions of the skin of the back and belly, connect the body with the wings, legs, and tail. Unlike birds, bats use both legs and wings during flight. Other modifications for flight include greatly elongated fingers to provide support for the wing membrane, a keeled sternum for the attachment of the enlarged flight muscles, and fusion of some vertebrae. The membrane extending from the tail to the hind legs is known as the interfemoral membrane.

The senses of sight and hearing are well developed in bats. Since most bats become active near dusk and are active much of the night, sight is of little importance in navigation and in the capture of prey. Instead, they use echolocation, a system somewhat similar to radar. They emit ultrasonic calls far above the range of human hearing that are reflected from objects ahead of them. They hear the echoes and are able to avoid obstacles and find food in total darkness. Different species can be distinguished by differences in the structure of their echolocation calls (Fenton and Bell, 1981).

During feeding maneuvers, the tail and wing membranes are used to capture and restrain prey. Some insects are captured by the tail membrane, which forms a pouch-like compartment. The bat must bend its head forward in order to grasp the insect with its teeth and take it into its mouth. Sometimes the bat may use its mouth to capture an insect from its wing.

Ten species of bats have been recorded in the park and all feed exclusively on insects. During the colder months when flying insects are unavailable, bats must either hibernate or migrate to warmer areas. Seven of our bats are known to hibernate. Only three — the red bat, hoary bat, and the silver-haired bat — are migratory. Bats have been seen flying over the park during every month of the year. When flying during the winter, however, they do not feed.

Mating in most hibernating species occurs from late August through October during the time of swarming at cave entrances. The spermatozoa are stored in the female's reproductive tract during the winter until ovulation occurs in the spring following arousal from hibernation. Only then do the stored sperm fertilize the ova released from the ovaries. This unusual process is known as delayed fertilization. A second mating may sometimes occur in the spring.

Most female bats give birth to one or two young annually. Female red bats, however, normally have three or four offspring. Some banded bats are known to have lived in the wild for more than 30 years.

Bats are capable of transmitting two diseases to humans - rabies and histoplasmosis. Histoplasmosis is a disease caused by inhaling dust that contains contaminated spores. Tuttle (1988) stated: "Less than a half of 1 percent of bats contract rabies, a frequency no higher than that seen in many other animals. Like others, they die quickly, but unlike even dogs and cats, rabid bats seldom become aggressive." Bats do not attack when they get rabies; they just lie in one place. Although it is rare for humans to contract rabies from infected bats, persons handling them should be aware of this possibility.

All of the park's caves provide critically important habitats for bats. A permit must be obtained in order to enter any cave in the park. Permits are issued only to qualified individuals and are not issued during periods of the year when females are rearing their young.

LITTLE BROWN MYOTIS
Myotis lucifugus

Tennessee — 1

Total Length : 3 – 4 in (75 – 98 mm)
Tail : 1 1/4 – 1 3/4 in (30 – 45 mm)
Weight : 1/4 – 1/3 oz (7 – 10 g)

Four of the ten species of bats in the park belong to the genus *Myotis*. They are difficult to distinguish from one another.

The little brown myotis is brownish. The hairs on the back have long, glossy tips that give the pelage a metallic sheen. The underparts are whitish or gray washed with buff. The ears, wings, and tail membranes are dark brown. The ear reaches to the tip of the nose when laid forward. Hairs on the hind feet extend beyond the toes.

During the summer, these bats are usually found in buildings, towers, hollow trees, beneath the loose bark of trees, in crevices of cliffs, and beneath bridges. During the winter, these colonial bats move into caves and abandoned mines where they either hang individually or in small clusters of 25 or 30.

Little brown myotis have only been recorded from eight localities in the park and along the Foothills Parkway: Myhr Cave (1,530 feet), Saltpeter Cave (1,750 feet), Bull Cave, Cataloochee, Elkmont, Greenbrier Cove (1,800 feet), Hazel Creek Ranger Station, and Blowhole Cave in Whiteoak Sink.

This species holds the record for longevity among bats — 32 years.

NORTHERN MYOTIS
Myotis septentrionalis

Tennessee — 1

Total Length : 3 – 4 in (75 – 100 mm)
Tail : 1 1/2 – 1 3/4 in (36 – 45 mm)
Weight : 1/6 – 1/3 oz (5 – 10 g)

Although similar to the little brown myotis in size and coloration, the northern myotis has duller pelage and larger ears which extend 4 to 5 mm beyond the tip of the nose when laid forward. The wing attaches along the side of the foot, reaching to the base of the toes.

These bats are found in caves, mines, buildings, hollow trees, under loose bark, and behind shutters. They roost singly or in small colonies. Individuals have been recorded near park headquarters; in Sugarlands; at Blowhole Cave in Whiteoak Sink; in Bull Cave; and at Myhr Cave.

The maximum recorded age for a wild individual is 18.5 years (Hall et al., 1957).

INDIANA MYOTIS [Endangered]
Myotis sodalis

Tennessee — 1

Total Length : 2 3/4 – 3 3/4 in (69 – 95 mm)
Tail : 1 – 1 3/4 in (25 – 45 mm)
Weight : 1/7 – 1/4 oz (4 – 8 g)

The dorsal pelage of the Indiana myotis differs from that of the other three species of *Myotis* in being somewhat tricolored. Each hair is black at its base, grayish in the middle, and has a cinnamon-brown tip. The belly hairs are grayish tinged with cinnamon-brown. Overall coloration is dull chestnut-gray above and pinkish-white beneath. The ear reaches the nostril when laid forward. Hairs on the toes barely reach the base of the claws.

These bats are most often taken in caves where they form dense masses on the ceilings and walls. Occasionally, individuals may be found in or on buildings. The Indiana myotis is included on the United States Fish and Wildlife Service's list of federally endangered native mammals. The distribution of this species is associated with major cave regions in the eastern United States from Vermont to Florida and west to Oklahoma and Wisconsin. However, it has shown a drastic decrease in population since 1950, and it is scarce in some parts of its range.

Harvey (1992) stated: "The present total population is estimated at less than 400,000, with more than 85 percent hibernating at only seven localities — two caves and a mine in Missouri, two caves in Indiana, and two caves in Kentucky. . . . estimates at major hibernacula indicated a 34 percent decline from 1983 to 1989."

The Indiana myotis was first recorded at park headquarters in 1937. In 1950, 2,242 individuals were counted in Blowhole Cave in Whiteoak Sink. In 1972, approximately 20,000 bats were observed; in 1975, 6,050 were present; in 1987, 10,760 bats were counted; in 1991, 5,383 bats were counted; and in 1993, 3,900 bats were present in the same cave. This represents the largest known population of this species in the state of Tennessee. Harvey (1991) noted that approximately 8,500 bats hibernate in Blowhole Cave and a small colony of approximately 200 Indiana myotis hibernate in Bull Cave. These are the only records for the park.

EASTERN SMALL-FOOTED MYOTIS
Myotis leibii

Tennessee — 2

Total Length : 2 7/8 – 3 1/4 in (72 – 83 mm)
Tail : 1 1/8 – 1 1/2 in (29 – 36 mm)
Weight : 1/10 – 1/3 oz (3 – 9 g)

The eastern small-footed myotis is the smallest member of the genus *Myotis* in North America. The fur is long, silky, and tan to golden-brown. The two main distinguishing characteristics are a distinct black mask across the face and the tiny feet that average only approximately 5/16 of an inch (7 to 8 mm) in length.

This species has been found most commonly in caves in forested areas. Some individuals have also been taken in rock crevices, beneath bridges, and in buildings.

This is among the rarest bats in the park. The first recorded individual was discovered in a cabin at Porter's Flat in Greenbrier Cove on April 24, 1970 at an elevation of approximately 2,200 feet (Neuhauser, 1971). On June 19, 1989, a second specimen was identified roosting in a building at park headquarters. It was measured, photographed, and released.

The longest recorded lifespan of a wild individual has been 12 years (Hitchcock, 1965; Kunz, 1982).

SILVER-HAIRED BAT
Lasionycteris noctivagans

Tennessee - North Carolina — 1, 2, 5

Total Length : 4 – 4 1/4 in (100 – 108 mm)
Tail : 1 1/4 – 1 3/4 in (30 – 42 mm)
Weight : 1/5 – 2/5 oz (6 – 14 g)

The silver-haired bat is a medium-sized bat with dark brownish-black fur. Many of the hairs on the back and on the interfemoral membrane are tipped with silvery-white. The ears are short and nearly as broad as they are long. When laid forward, the ears barely reach the nostrils. The basal half of the dorsal surface of the interfemoral membrane is sparsely furred.

This is a solitary, migratory bat. The pattern of flight has a distinctive fluttery quality with frequent darts, twists, and glides. It is most commonly found in hollow trees or beneath the bark of trees. Occasionally, individuals may be found in caves and in buildings.

This species has been recorded from only nine localities in the park: Cades Cove (2,000 feet), Greenbrier, Whiteoak Sink, park headquarters, Deep Creek Ranger Station (1,900 feet), and Meigs Creek (2,500 feet). In 1962, the first and only high altitude record resulted from the discovery of a dead bat on the Appalachian Trail between Newfound Gap and Indian Gap.

Silver-haired bats breed in the northern part of the United States and Canada and then migrate southward in fall. No young have been reported from the park.

were usually "jumped" from rhododendron thickets near the summits of the peaks. Kellogg's record is listed by Hall (1981) as being a marginal record for the species. Blair et al (1968) also give the range as extending "south in Appalachian chain to eastern Tennessee." Smith, Funderburg, and Quay (1960) state that this species probably occurs in open brushy areas in mixed forests in the mountains of Virginia and Tennessee. Stupka is convinced that this hare is not here now, and he doubts that it was here in pre-Park days." As recently as 1982, Bittner and Rongstad reported the hare's range as ". . . extending south through the Allegheny Mountain Range into North Carolina and Tennessee."

EASTERN COTTONTAIL
Sylvilagus floridanus

Tennessee - North Carolina — 1, 2, 3, 4, 5, 6

Total Length : 13 – 20 in (320 – 500 mm)
Tail : 1 5/8 – 3 in (40 – 75 mm)
Weight : 2 – 4 lbs (.9 – 1.8 kg)

The eastern cottontail is a medium-sized rabbit in which the nape of the neck is rusty. The dorsal coloration varies from reddish-brown to grayish-brown sprinkled with black. The ears are dark grayish-tan bordered with black. The underparts are grayish-white except for the chest which is brownish. The short, fluffy tail is brownish above and white below.

Cottontail rabbits are found in a variety of habitats including old fields, brushy clearings, brier patches, hedgerows, orchards, and along the edges of woodlands. In the park, eastern cottontails range from the lowest elevations to Mount LeConte and Clingman's Dome.

These rabbits are solitary except during the breeding season when each female produces several litters. Most breeding in the park probably occurs between March and August. Young have been observed in May and June and half-grown cottontails have been recorded in July and September. Most cottontails die before they are a year old, but there are reports of wild individuals reaching five and seven years of age.

Eastern cottontails are preyed on by many predators, including snakes, hawks, owls, and carnivorous mammals. Specific predators recorded within the park include black rat snakes and timber rattlesnakes (Savage, 1967; Linzey and Linzey, 1971).

APPALACHIAN COTTONTAIL
Sylvilagus obscurus

Tennessee — 2, 3

Total Length : 14 – 18 in (350 – 450 mm)
Tail : 1 5/8 – 2 1/8 in (40 – 52 mm)
Weight : 2 – 3 1/4 lbs (.9 – 1.5 kg)

This species was formerly known as the New England cottontail (*Sylvilagus transitionalis*) (Linzey and Linzey, 1971). It was reclassified by Chapman et al. (1992).

The Appalachian cottontail closely resembles the eastern cottontail in size and color. It differs only in its slightly smaller size, shorter ears, and greater amount of black on the back. A narrow black patch is present on top of the head between the ears. The rufous or rusty nape patch characteristic of the eastern cottontail is lacking. Due to the similarity of these two forms, most park records refer simply to "cottontail."

This is a secretive, forest-dwelling rabbit that is never abundant over most of its range. It inhabits woods, shrubby areas, and brushy areas. It prefers thicker wooded cover than the eastern cottontail.

Kellogg (1939) recorded the first specimen from the park near Low Gap (3,300 feet). Two additional specimens — one from Pine Knot Branch near Elkmont (2,100 feet) in 1957 and one from the Alum Cave parking area (3,800 feet) in 1960 — are the only other park records.

CHIPMUNKS, WOODCHUCKS, AND SQUIRRELS
Family Sciuridae

The seven members of this family occurring in the park are diverse in habits and habitat. Some live on the ground, such as the woodchuck and eastern chipmunk, whereas others, such as the eastern gray squirrel and the red squirrel, spend most of their time in trees. Most are active during the day (diurnal), but the flying squirrels are active at night (nocturnal). Some are active all year; others hibernate. Plant food forms the bulk of the diet of most species. Green vegetation and a variety of seeds, including acorns and nuts, are the primary foods.

All rodents have chisel-like incisor teeth that are specialized for gnawing. Canine teeth are absent. A diastema is present.

EASTERN CHIPMUNK
Tamias striatus

Tennessee - North Carolina — 1, 2, 3, 4, 5, 6

Total Length : 8 3/4 – 10 in (220 – 255 mm)
Tail : 3 – 4 in (75 – 100 mm)
Weight : 2 1/2 – 5 oz (70 – 140 g)

The eastern chipmunk is reddish-brown with five conspicuous dark dorsal stripes. The underparts are white. The tail is well-haired, the ears are prominent and rounded, and internal cheek pouches are present.

The Cherokee Indians have an interesting legend accounting for the chipmunk's stripes. Chamberlain (1963) related the following: "After man had invented weapons, and began to hunt and kill the animals, birds, etc., the latter held a grand council to decide how to retaliate. After considerable discussion, it was determined that each of the creatures in question should visit upon man some disease or sickness; and this is why mankind is now subject to such afflictions. One alone, of all the animals, said he had no quarrel with man, and spoke against the retaliation proposed. This was the little ground-squirrel, whose action so incensed the other animals that they fell upon him and sought to tear him to pieces. He escaped, however, but bears the marks of the struggle to this very day."

Chipmunks prefer deciduous hardwood forests, especially rocky areas, the edges of grass balds and clearings, and farmlands. They can climb well but spend most of their time on the ground. Chipmunks occur throughout the park from Cades Cove, Deep Creek, Smokemont, Elkmont, the Foothills Parkway, and Cosby to Mount Guyot and Clingmans Dome. Although recorded from such areas as Mount Guyot and Clingmans Dome, they are much less abundant in the spruce-fir forests.

Eastern chipmunks live a solitary existence most of the year, although family groups may sometimes overwinter together. Chipmunks may become inactive during periods of high temperatures in summer and during severe winter weather. Even though in some regions they enter into a deep sleep, they do not store fat and must awaken periodically to feed on stored food. Occasionally, active chipmunks may be observed when snow is on the ground. Chipmunks have been seen during every month of the year in the park.

Food consists chiefly of nuts such as acorns, hickory nuts, beechnuts, and walnuts; small seeds; berries; wild grapes; and a variety of small animal life including snails, earthworms, and insects. Much food is stored during late summer and fall. The large internal cheek pouches are used for transporting food to underground storage chambers or other cache sites. The cheek pouch of one chipmunk examined in the park contained a wild grape.

Litters averaging three to five young are born in early spring and in mid-summer. The life span in the wild is probably between two and four years, although some have lived at least eight years.

Eastern chipmunks may be captured by a variety of predators including snakes, hawks, foxes, bobcats, and weasels. Known predators in the park include black rat snakes and timber rattlesnakes.

WOODCHUCK
Marmota monax

Tennessee - North Carolina — 1, 2, 3, 4, 5, 6

Total Length : 22 – 27 in (550 – 675 mm)
Tail : 4 – 7 in (100 – 175 mm)
Weight : 5 – 10 lbs (2.25 – 4.50 kg)

The short-legged woodchuck is a large, stocky rodent with a broad, flattened head, a blunt nose, and a medium-length tail. It is the largest member of its family in the park.

Also known as "groundhog" and "whistle-pig," the woodchuck has long, coarse yellowish-brown to brown fur that has a grizzled, or slightly frosted, appearance because of the presence of whitish, buff, or cinnamon-colored hairs. Whitish areas are present on the sides of the face, nose, lips, and chin. The feet are dark brown to black. The flattened tail is furred and varies in color from black to dark brown. The underparts are whitish-buff to brownish.

In the park, woodchucks have been seen from the lowest elevations to approximately 6,300 feet (Forney Ridge). They are most abundant, however, in the open meadowlands and along the mowed roadsides at the lower elevations. They are rare in dense forests and in the spruce-fir region. The ecological changes occurring in the park as it reverts to a forested condition has decreased suitable habitat for the woodchuck, and it is less plentiful now than formerly.

Woodchucks are solitary and are most active in early morning and late afternoon. They dig their own burrows, each of which may have as many as five entrances. Abandoned burrows, or burrows containing a hibernating woodchuck, may be used by snakes, opossums, cottontails, skunks, weasels, foxes, and other wildlife.

Woodchucks have excellent eyesight and are able to climb trees in order to escape an enemy. When startled, a woodchuck will give a loud, shrill whistle; hence the name "whistle-pig."

By the end of summer, woodchucks have become very fat in preparation for hibernation. Although active woodchucks have been recorded in the park during every month, most enter hibernation. Entrance into hibernation is apparently caused by decreasing daylength. A hibernating woodchuck is coiled into a tight ball with the head resting on its lower abdomen and the hind parts and tail wrapped over the head. During this deep sleep, respiration and heartbeat are greatly decreased, and body temperature is considerably lower than when the animal was active. In general, the metabolic rate of animals in hibernation is between 1/30 and 1/100 of the "resting" metabolic rate of non-hibernating animals. During hibernation, the breathing rate may be reduced to only one breath every five or six minutes, while the woodchuck's heartbeats may be as few as three beats per minute, in contrast to the normal rate of 80 to 95 beats per minute. Rectal temperature reaches a low of 3°C (38°F) during hibernation, while the normal summer reading is 32°C (90°F).

Woodchucks feed primarily on grasses, clover, alfalfa, wheat, corn, soybeans, and berries. Bark may occasionally be consumed.

Young are usually born during April and May. Litter size may range from two to nine, but usually consists of three to five. Woodchucks have been known to live five to six years in the wild.

Although woodchucks are well protected by their alertness and their burrows, some are taken by bobcats, bears, foxes, weasels, and rattlesnakes. Stupka found a woodchuck recently killed by a bobcat above Big Cove (3,200 feet), an area just outside the park boundary in North Carolina. Many woodchucks are killed by automobiles.

GRAY SQUIRREL
Sciurus carolinensis

Tennessee - North Carolina — 1, 2, 3, 4, 5

Total Length : 16 – 22 in (400 – 550 mm)
Tail : 6 1/2 – 10 in (170 – 255 mm)
Weight : 1 – 2 1/4 lbs (360 – 650 g)

The medium-sized, bushy-tailed gray squirrel has primarily gray upperparts and silvery-gray underparts. The head, midback, sides, and upper surfaces of the feet are washed with yellowish-brown. A whitish ring is present around each eye, and white is present on the backs of the ears. Both albinistic (white) and melanistic (black) individuals have been recorded in the park.

Gray squirrels prefer dense hardwood and mixed coniferous-hardwood forests, especially oak and beech woods. Although they have been observed at all elevations in the park, they are rare in the spruce-fir zone. Ravines, slopes, and river bottoms provide especially suitable habitat.

Gray squirrels spend most of their time in trees. They come to the ground mainly to find food. Foraging for food takes place primarily in early morning and late afternoon. The acorns, nuts, buds, and fruits of oaks, hickories, black gum, and beech provide the important year-round staple foods. These food items are supplemented during certain seasons by the buds, flowers, and fruits of trees such as dogwood, silverbell, buckeye, and American hornbeam; corn; mushrooms; and insects.

Nests are constructed of leaves and twigs. They may be bulky structures in the crotch of a limb, or they may be in a cavity of a tree. Although gray squirrels are active during all seasons, they may remain in their nests for several days at a time during periods of severe weather. During the winter, several squirrels may occupy a single den cavity. On January 24, 1935, four squirrels were found in a single den in a dead chestnut tree.

Female gray squirrels usually produce two litters annually. Average litter size is two to three. Life spans up to 12 1/2 years have been recorded in natural populations.

Recorded instances of predation in the park include the timber rattlesnake and the bobcat (Linzey and Linzey, 1971). A number of squirrels are killed every year by automobiles on park roads. This number greatly increases during years of hard mast shortages or failures.

FOX SQUIRREL
Sciurus niger

Tennessee - North Carolina — 1, 2, 3

Total Length : 19 – 28 in (475 – 700 mm)
Tail : 10 – 15 in (250 – 390 mm)
Weight : 1 1/4 – 3 1/4 lbs (0.6 – 1.5 kg)

The fox squirrel is the largest tree squirrel in the park. Most individuals are rusty brown with a blackish head and a white nose. The underparts and tail are normally orange or yellow.

Fox squirrels prefer higher ground and larger trees than gray squirrels. Open, mature stands of pine or mixed stands of pine, oak, and sweetgum form ideal habitat. Areas with a minimum of underbrush are preferred. Fox squirrels avoid the cutover areas and young growth preferred by gray squirrels.

Fox squirrels are rarely seen in the park. They have been reported along the Foothills Parkway at Mill Creek (2,000 to 2,400 feet), Bradley Fork (about 2,500 feet), along Little River Road between park headquarters and Fighting Creek Gap, between Eagle and Hazel creeks (near Proctor), near Shuckstack Tower (4,000 feet), and at Wear Cove near the park boundary.

Fox squirrels are not as agile in trees as are gray squirrels, but they are fast and graceful when running on the ground. Like gray squirrels, they are diurnal and are active during all seasons. Nests may be outside or in a tree cavity. Woodpecker holes are sometimes used for nests.

Food consists of acorns, nuts, seeds, buds, twigs, bark, berries, fruits, corn, seeds, mushrooms, and insects. An individual along Bradley Fork was observed eating mulberries (Linzey and Linzey, 1971). Much food is hoarded for use at a later date.

Females may have one or two litters a year. Average litters consist of two to four young. In the wild, marked fox squirrels have lived to an age of 12.6 years.

RED SQUIRREL
Tamiasciurus hudsonicus

Tennessee - North Carolina — 1, 2, 3, 4, 5, 6

Total Length : 10 – 14 in (250 – 350 mm)
Tail : 4 – 6 in (100 – 150 mm)
Weight : 7 – 8 3/4 oz (200 – 250 g)

The red squirrel is a common inhabitant of the park and has been observed at all elevations. The dorsal pelage is reddish-gray and the underparts are whitish. During the summer a black stripe is present along each side of the body. Ear tufts are present in winter.

The solitary red squirrel, locally known as "mountain boomer," is active during the day throughout the year. The nest of shredded bark and grasses is usually located in a natural tree cavity or a woodpecker hole. Food includes seeds, nuts, mushrooms, buds, and fruits such as blackberries. In the park, squirrels have been observed feeding on the fruits of cucumber tree, mountain holly, American chestnut, buckeye, black walnut, silverbell, beech, and serviceberry; and on the seeds of mountain maple, hemlock, pine, fir, and spruce. In April, 1938, Stupka observed a squirrel feeding on the sap of a yellow birch. These squirrels occasionally raid bird's nests and consume the eggs and/or nestling birds. In 1952, an individual was found near Newfound Gap eating a nestling red-breasted nuthatch (Grimes, 1952).

Females may produce litters of two to seven young in spring and summer. Some squirrels have lived as long as nine years.

Linzey and Linzey (1971) reported an interesting account between a red squirrel and a park Ranger: "On August 22, 1955, a nest containing six young Red Squirrels was found in a hollow limb of a large yellow birch at approximately 4500 ft. along the transmountain road (Tennessee). The young squirrels were less than half the size of adults and had proportionately large heads and feet. Three of the young were adopted by Park Ranger John Morrell, who took them to his home in their nest of thin, yellow birch bark. The young squirrels grew rapidly on their diet of condensed milk and warm water four times a day. On the third day, one individual had its eyes open and, on the following day, the eyes of the other two were open. According to Palmer (1954), this would indicate that the squirrels were 23 or 24 days old at the time of their capture, and the date of their birth would be approximately the last day of July. Apparently, this represents a second litter. By November 10, two of the three animals had died. On that day the remaining squirrel, named Rufus, was liberated at the lower edge of the spruce-fir forest, a few miles from where he was born. This animal had lived with the Morrells for a period of 80 days. The story of Rufus does not end here, however. From November 23, 1955, to January 6, 1957 — a period of more than 13 months — Mr. Morrell revisited 42 times the place where Rufus had been liberated. On 34 of these occasions, contact was made between man and squirrel. Mr. Morrell would call the animal's name, and ordinarily in a matter of some minutes the squirrel would put in his appearance. Usually he accepted food from the hand of his benefactor. A second Red Squirrel occasionally accompanied Rufus on visits beginning January 22, 1956. On July 1, 1956, both squirrels accepted food from Mr. Morrell. Final contact was made on January 6, 1957, after which Rufus could not be located."

SOUTHERN FLYING SQUIRREL
Glaucomys volans

Tennessee - North Carolina — 1, 2, 3, 4

Total Length : 8 – 10 1/2 in (200 – 265 mm)
Tail : 3 3/8 – 4 1/2 in (85 – 115 mm)
Weight : 1 1/2 – 3 oz (45 – 85 g)

Southern flying squirrels are small nocturnal tree squirrels with large eyes and a broad, flattened, well-furred tail. The brownish dorsal pelage is fine, soft, and dense. The hairs of the underparts are whitish or cream to their base in contrast to the hairs of the northern flying squirrel in which the basal portion of the hair is gray. A loose fold of furred skin connects the front and hind limbs from the wrists to the ankles.

These squirrels cannot fly. Rather, they glide from a higher perch to a lower one. In doing so, they spread their legs, thus drawing taut the loose skin running along each side of the body. The membranes support the squirrel as it glides in somewhat the same fashion as a parachute. The tail acts as a rudder. By varying the tension on their membranes and by altering the position of their tail, flying squirrels can control their direction and speed to some extent. They always land in a head-up position on the trunk of a tree.

Southern flying squirrels prefer areas with large deciduous trees, although they have also been taken in mixed deciduous-pine woodlands. They usually nest in tree cavities, but may occasionally build a leaf nest in the fork of a tree limb or move into a bird house or the attic of a home.

Southern flying squirrels have been recorded at elevations ranging from 1,500 to 1,600 feet (Foothills Parkway at Buena Vista) to 4,700 feet (Snake Den Mountain). Other localities include Abrams Branch, Big Creek, Deep Creek (2,200 feet), Greenbrier (2,500 feet), Smokemont (3,000 feet), Walnut Bottom (3,100 feet), and Blanket Mountain.

Flying squirrels are active throughout the year, although they may remain inactive for several weeks at a time during severe winter weather. In the park, active individuals have been observed every month. In December, 1940, 26 squirrels were found in one hollow chestnut tree (Linzey and Linzey, 1971).

Southern flying squirrels apparently have two litters annually in the park since a female taken on August 4 in Cades Cove contained four nearly full-term embryos. Average litter size is between two and four. Although southern flying squirrels have lived 13 years in captivity, the life expectancy in the wild is five to six years.

Female flying squirrels will go to great lengths to retrieve their young. While studying golden mice in the park, my wife and I investigated a leaf nest in the fork of a tree limb eight to ten feet above the ground. The nest contained four young flying squirrels who were fully haired but whose eyes had not yet opened. Since I had dislodged the nest in order to examine it, we temporarily placed the nest with the young squirrels in a box while deciding what to do with them. Within a few minutes, the female appeared and, with no hesitation, hopped into the box, picked up one baby, and carried it off. As we watched from a short distance away, she returned for each of the young. She was so intent on retrieving her young that we were able to take several photographs at close range. As we watched, she made two long glides following exactly the same route each time. She apparently took the babies to an alternate nest site. Others have also reported this strong maternal instinct for retrieving young. There are reports of females climbing up the leg of an observer to remove the babies from his hand and even removing them from a pocket. This behavior is most intense when the young are very small and diminishes as they approach weaning age.

The only predator on the southern flying squirrel ever recorded from within the park has been the timber rattlesnake (Stupka, 1960; Savage, 1967). Just outside the park, black rat snakes have been observed attempting to enter a bluebird house containing flying squirrels.

NORTHERN FLYING SQUIRREL
[Endangered]
Glaucomys sabrinus

Tennessee — 4, 5

Total Length : 10 – 11 in (255 – 275 mm)
Tail : 4 – 5 1/4 in (100 – 130 mm)
Weight : 4 – 6 1/2 oz (110 – 185 g)

Except for being larger, the northern flying squirrel appears similar to the southern flying squirrel. Both have brownish upperparts and whitish underparts. Whereas the belly hairs on the southern flying squirrel are white to their base, the bases of the belly hairs of the northern flying squirrel are usually grayish. The tail appears to be dorsoventrally flattened.

Preferred habitat consists of spruce-fir forests and mixed conifer-northern hardwood forests. In the southern Appalachians, these nocturnal squirrels feed mostly on lichens, mushrooms, seeds, buds, fruit, conifer cones, meat, and arthropods (Weigl, 1977).

Northern flying squirrels are uncommon in the park. The first individual was taken on Blanket Mountain (4,000 feet) on February 20, 1935. The habitat was deciduous forest "at least seven airline miles from the nearest spruce and fir" (Handley, 1953). Other individuals have been noted along Walker Prong, at Indian Gap, and at Newfound Gap. This species has been officially classified as Endangered in the southern Appalachians by the United States Fish and Wildlife Service.

Northern flying squirrels use shredded yellow birch bark, moss, and grass to construct their nests which are usually in a tree cavity or a woodpecker hole. Occasionally, outside nests are used. Litters may be produced in spring and midsummer and usually consist of two to five young. Life expectancy in the wild is probably less than four years.

BEAVERS

Family Castoridae

Beavers are the largest rodents native to North America. Some individuals may occasionally weigh 50 pounds (22.5 kg) or more. The broad, flat, scaly tail is a key identification feature.

AMERICAN BEAVER
Castor canadensis

North Carolina — 1, 2

Total Length : 36 – 60 in (900 – 1,200 mm)
Tail : 9 – 12 in (225 – 300 mm)
Weight : 29 – 49 lbs (13.5 – 22 kg)

Beavers are brown to blackish-brown with slightly paler underparts. The dense pelage consists of fine, short underfur overlaid with long, coarse, shiny guard hairs. The ears are small and are set far back on the broad, rounded head. The flattened tail and webbed hind feet are black. Both the ears and the nose are equipped with valves that shut when the animal is underwater. The heavy, broad incisor teeth are dark orange-chestnut on their anterior surfaces.

Beavers are primarily found along streams in areas with sufficient food and where conditions are suitable for building a dam to form a pond.

The history of beavers in the park was summarized by Linzey and Linzey (1971): "Although this species was widespread in former times, there had been no evidence of its occurrence within the area now encompassed by the Park until 1966. In 1896, Rhoads stated: "It is not likely that any beavers now exist in the eastern half of the State [Tennessee]." In discussing the status of the beaver in North Carolina, Brimley (1945) stated that it was "apparently extinct," being last recorded from Stokes County about 1897.

and surrounded by a pile of sticks and twigs that may be up to nine feet in diameter and four to five feet high. The debris heap may consist of eight to ten bushels or more of material. Most nests are on the ground, but near Chambers Creek a woodrat was found in a nest 10 feet above ground in a dense growth of privet.

The senses of smell, sight, hearing, and touch are well developed. Drumming has been observed in woodrats.

Food consists primarily of fruits, berries, nuts, seeds, bark, and grasses. Individuals in the park are known to have fed on pokeweed berries. A dead woodrat had a 2-inch sprig of poison ivy with berries in its mouth.

Several litters consisting of two to four young are produced from spring to fall. A nest containing a nursing female and two blind young approximately ten days old was found on August 14, 1950, at Abrams Creek Ranger Station. Two very small immature individuals were recorded at Big Creek during the period October 1 – 4, 1950. Woodrats have survived 33 months in the wild.

SOUTHERN RED-BACKED VOLE
Clethrionomys gapperi

Tennessee - North Carolina — 1, 2, 3, 4, 5, 6

Total Length : 4 3/4 – 6 1/2 in (120 – 165 mm)
Tail : 1 3/8 – 2 in (35 -- 50 mm)
Weight : 1/2 – 1 1/2 oz (14 – 42 g)

The southern red-backed vole is a small, moderately short-tailed mouse with a reddish back, grayish sides, and a silvery belly. The fur is generally longer and more dense in winter than in summer. The tail is bicolored.

Red-backed voles prefer cool, damp areas in coniferous, deciduous, or mixed forests. Ideal habitat includes moss-covered logs and rocks, deep crevices among boulders on hillsides, along small boulder-strewn streams, and rhododendron thickets.

Although they have been found in the park at elevations ranging from 1,750 to 6,620 feet, they are most abundant in the spruce-fir forests. Localities include Sutton Ridge near Cosby (1,750 feet), Kanati Fork (2,800 feet), West Prong of the Little Pigeon River along the Newfound Gap Road (3,400 feet, 4,000 feet), Buck Prong (3,500 to 5,000 feet), Eagle Rock Creek (3,600 feet), Greenbrier Cove (4,100 to 4,600 feet), Low Gap (4,242 feet), Chapman Prong (5,000 feet), Walker Prong, Bote Mountain (4,700 feet),

Indian Gap (4,800 feet, 5,200 feet), Mount Collins (5,000 feet), Newfound Gap, Silers Bald, Spence Field, Collins Gap (5,800 feet), Mount Kephart (6,200 feet), Clingmans Dome (6,300 to 6,642 feet), and Mount Guyot (6,000 to 6,620 feet).

Red-backed voles may be active at any time of the day or night and during all seasons of the year. Food consists of green vegetation, bark, fungi, seeds, nuts, and invertebrates.

Breeding occurs during the spring and summer months with litters normally consisting of four to six young. Maximum longevity is approximately 20 months.

The only known predator of this species in the park is the timber rattlesnake (Savage, 1967).

MEADOW VOLE
Microtus pennsylvanicus

North Carolina — 2

Total Length : 5 – 7 1/2 in (125 – 190 mm)
Tail : 1 2/5 – 2 3/5 in (38 – 63 mm)
Weight : 1 – 2 1/2 oz (28 – 70 g)

Meadow voles are dark brown to brownish-gray with silvery-gray underparts. The small ears are partially hidden in the fur. The short tail is usually less than half as long as the head and body combined. The eyes are small and black.

This open grassland species is most often found in old fields, orchards, and low, moist areas near streams and rivers. R. J. Fleetwood reported finding meadow vole runways along Forney Creek at the mouth of Jonas Creek in 1934 and on the Cherokee Indian Reservation near the park boundary. It was not until December, 1965, however, that the only meadow vole recorded from the park was taken by the author and his wife (Linzey and Linzey, 1967). The juvenile female was taken in a marshy field along the Oconaluftee River near the Smokemont Campground in North Carolina.

These voles are active at all hours during all seasons. Food consists primarily of green vegetation during the warmer months, supplemented by bark and roots during the winter. Meadow voles are known to ingest fecal pellets (coprophagy).

Female meadow voles are prolific breeders. Litters of three to five young may be born during any month. Females may be able to breed when approximately 25 days old. One female is known to have produced 17 litters in one year. Most meadow voles live only three to six months, although there are some records of wild individuals living for 18 months. They serve as prey for a large variety of predators.

ROCK VOLE
Microtus chrotorrhinus

Tennessee - North Carolina — 2, 3, 4, 5, 6

Total Length : 5 1/2 – 7 in (140 – 175 mm)
Tail : 1 3/8 – 2 in (35 – 51 mm)
Weight : 1 – 2 oz (25 – 57 g)

Rock voles are medium-sized, brownish above and grayish-white below. The area between the nostrils and the eyes usually ranges from yellowish — to deep orange-rufous, a condition that may be obvious in some specimens, but inconspicuous or lacking in others.

In the park, rock voles are found primarily among mossy rocks and logs or in cool, moist talus areas. They utilize a network of runways beneath and between the rocks and boulders. They may be active any time during the day or night and during all seasons.

Rock voles were first discovered and named by Komarek (1932). The first specimens were taken in the Great Smoky Mountains National Park. They are fairly common in areas above 3,000 feet elevation and often occur in association with the southern red-backed vole. Localities in the park include Indian Camp Creek (2,650 feet), Kanati Fork (2,800 feet), Bradley Fork (3,200 feet), Buck Prong, Chimneys Campground, Smokemont (3,000 to 3,200 feet), Fort Harry Cliffs (3,200 feet), Greenbrier Cove (3,500 to 4,000 feet), Walker Prong (3,700 feet), Eagle Rock Creek (3,500 feet), Oconaluftee River (3,800 feet), Grassy Patch (4,000 feet), Mingus Mill Creek (4,000 feet), West Prong of the Little Pigeon River, Buck Fork (4,200 feet), Spence Field (5,500 feet), Newfound Gap, Indian Gap (5,200 feet), Pecks Corner (5,500 feet), Thunderhead (5,400 feet), Silers Bald (5,620 feet), Andrews Bald (5,800 feet), and Mount Kephart (6,200 feet).

Food consists primarily of green vegetation, roots, and berries. Breeding extends from early spring into fall. Several litters consisting of an average of three young each are produced annually.

Predators identified in the park include a bobcat which contained five rock voles, timber rattlesnakes, and copperheads (Savage, 1967; Linzey and Linzey, 1971).

WOODLAND VOLE
Microtus pinetorum

Tennessee - North Carolina — 1, 2, 3, 4, 5

Total Length : 4 – 5 3/4 in (100 – 145 mm)
Tail : 5/8 – 3/4 in (18 – 20 mm)
Weight : 3/4 – 2 oz (21 – 56 g)

The fossorial woodland vole is brownish above and grayish below. The fur is soft and thick and lies flat against the body when rubbed either forward or backward, an adaptation for traveling either direction in tunnels. The nose is blunt, and the short tail is only slightly longer than the small hind feet. The eyes and ears are small with the ears being partially concealed in the fur.

Woodland voles may be found in moist woodlands, orchards, fields, and gardens. Optimum habitat includes light moist soil or deep humus and a heavy ground cover.

Most park records are below 2,000 feet, although woodland voles have been taken as high as 5,000 feet (Spence Field). The Komareks took these voles in an open deciduous woods in Cades Cove where the mice had runways under a layer of dead leaves. In Greenbrier Cove, specimens were taken in an apple orchard and in a small marshy area at the edge of a woods (Komarek and Komarek, 1938). At Deep Creek (2,000 feet), woodland voles were taken in a sedge field bordered on one side with pines and on the other with oaks and shrubs. Other localities include Cove Creek (1,430 feet), Cove Spring Hollow (1,500 feet), King Hollow Branch (1,700 to 1,800 feet), Cosby (1,750 feet), Indian Creek (2,000 feet), Elkmont, Cherokee Orchard (2,400 feet), and Cataloochee (2,600 feet).

Woodland voles are active during all seasons. More activity normally occurs at night than during the daylight hours.

Woodland voles may construct their own burrows just beneath the leaf mold, or they may use mole burrow systems. Nests of dead leaves, grasses, plant stems, and rootlets are usually located in the underground burrow, but occasionally may be beneath a stump or log. The senses of hearing and touch are extremely well developed.

Roots, tubers, stems, bark, fruits, and seeds comprise the major portion of the diet, although occasionally some insects may be consumed. Grass, decomposed apples, and kernels of corn were found in runways by the Komareks. Some food may be stored in underground chambers for use during the winter.

Breeding occurs from late winter well into November. Females containing embryos or nursing females have been recorded in March, September, and December. Litters usually consist of one to three young. Wild individuals have been known to live as long as 18 months.

Corn snakes and copperheads are the only known predators in the park.

SOUTHERN BOG LEMMING
Synaptomys cooperi

Tennessee - North Carolina — 1, 2, 3, 4, 5
Total Length: 4 – 5 1/2 in (100 – 138 mm)
Tail : 3/5 – 7/8 in (15 – 22 mm)
Weight : 1/2 – 1 2/5 oz (14 – 42 g)

The small, short-legged southern bog lemming is brownish-gray above and grayish below. The short tail is less than one inch long, and the massive head contains small ears that are nearly concealed in the fur. Each broad upper incisor has a shallow groove near its outer edge.

Southern bog lemmings have been taken in grassy openings in woods, among mossy boulders in spruce forests, in bogs, in clearcuts, pastures, and power line rights-of-way. In the park, they are found most commonly at the higher elevations, although they have been recorded as low as 1,400 feet at Greenbrier. Individuals taken by the Komareks were found in "small scattered grassy patches throughout the mountains." Localities include Roaring Fork, between Forney Creek and Jonas Creek (2,400 feet), Cataloochee, Kanati Fork (2,800 feet), Little River (2,900 feet), Elkmont (2,900 feet), Grassy Patch (4,000 feet), Spence Field (5,000 feet), Indian Gap (5,200 feet), and Silers Bald (5,620 feet).

Southern bog lemmings are primarily nocturnal and are active all year. They construct both surface and underground runways. Food consists primarily of green vegetation. Fruits and fungi may be taken occasionally.

Southern bog lemmings breed from February to November. The Komareks recorded females containing from one to four embryos in various stages of development during March. Most wild individuals probably survive less than one year.

<hr />

MUSKRAT
Ondatra zibethicus

Tennessee - North Carolina — 1, 2, 3, 4, 5

Total Length : 21 1/4 – 25 in (545 – 640 mm)
Tail : 9 3/4 – 11 in (250 – 283 mm)
Weight : 1 1/3 – 4 lbs (.6 – 1.8 kg)

The muskrat is a large semi-aquatic rodent. The upperparts are covered with soft, dense, glossy brown underfur and reddish-brown or black guard hairs. The underparts are whitish or pale brown. The eyes and ears are small, and the hind feet are partially webbed. The tail is long, sparsely haired, and laterally compressed. The hind feet and tail serve as oars and a rudder when swimming. Orange enamel covers the front surfaces of the large incisor teeth. The lips are able to close behind the incisor teeth so that the muskrat can gnaw while underwater.

Muskrats possess a pair of musk glands which enlarge during the breeding season, especially in males. These glands emit a musky yellowish secretion. The name muskrat is derived from this musky odor and the animal's ratlike appearance.

In the park, muskrats are found primarily in the larger streams and are fairly common below 2,400 feet. Localities include Abrams Creek, Greenbrier Cove (1,350 feet), Cades Cove (1,800 feet), Cosby (2,400 feet), near Gatlinburg, Elkmont, Bradley Fork, the Oconaluftee River, Deep Creek, Forney Creek, and Indian Creek. Park records, however, contain two unusual high elevation records. A young muskrat was observed on the Rainbow Falls Trail (5,300 feet) in April, 1949 (Tanner, personal communication to Stupka, April 28, 1949). In March, 1951, an individual was found dead on the Tennessee side of the Newfound Gap Road (4,500 feet) (Stupka). It is thought that these were wandering individuals.

Muskrats are usually more active during the night than during the day and are active during all seasons. They may build houses of sticks, grasses, rushes, leaves, and mud, or they may excavate a burrow in the bank. Houses may range from 3 to 9 feet in diameter at the base and rise 2 to 4 feet above the surface of the water. Each house has one or more underwater entrances and one or more dry chambers.

Muskrats are primarily vegetarians and feed on the stems, leaves, and roots of many plants. Their diet may also occasionally include crayfish, other invertebrates, fish, frogs or turtles.

Most muskrats are born during April and May, although some breeding also occurs in August and September. Most litters consist of three to five young. Although the mortality rate of young muskrats is quite high, some wild individuals have been known to live for four years.

Predators may include raccoons, mink, otters, foxes, hawks, snakes, and snapping turtles. No specific records of predation have been noted in the park.

BLACK RAT
Rattus rattus

Tennessee - North Carolina — 1, 2, 3, 4, 5, 6

Total Length : 12 1/2 – 16 1/2 in (325 – 425 mm)
Tail : 7 1/2 – 9 1/2 in (190 – 240 mm)
Weight : 5 – 10 oz (140 – 280 g)

The black rat is a non-native (exotic) species that is thought to have arrived in North America in the mid-1500s on the ships of early European explorers. It is native to Asia Minor and the Orient (Walker, 1964).

The black rat is a medium-sized, slender brownish- or grayish-black rat with coarse fur and a long, sparsely haired, scaly tail. The tail is longer (approximately 110 percent) than the combined length of the head and body. This feature serves as a key identification character in differentiating this species from the Norway rat. The underparts are grayish-white.

The black rat is found primarily around human habitations such as barns, warehouses, and buildings in urban residential areas. Although recorded from a wide range of elevations in the park, it is now an uncommon resident. It was formerly reported to be abundant around barns in Greenbrier Cove (1,680 to 2,000 feet) by Komarek and Komarek (1938), but it is now much more scarce. Individuals have been recorded at park headquarters, along Little River near Metcalf Bottoms (1,800 feet), Elkmont (2,150 feet), and Smokemont (2,200 feet). The highest elevation recorded in the park was on July 24, 1941 when an individual was taken on the summit of Mount LeConte (6,300 feet).

Black rats are mainly nocturnal and are active all year. They feed on a variety of plant and animal items. Food may include garbage, grain, seeds, meat, insects, and green vegetation.

In the park, breeding probably occurs throughout the warmer months with females producing litters averaging five or six young . Some individuals have lived over a year in the wild.

NORWAY RAT
Rattus norvegicus

Tennessee - North Carolina — 1, 2, 3, 4, 5, 6

Total Length : 12 1/2 – 18 1/2 in (325 – 475 mm)
Tail : 5 3/4 – 8 1/2 in (150 – 215 mm)
Weight : 10 – 11 3/4 oz (280 – 335 g)

The Norway rat is a non-native (exotic) species that is thought to have arrived in North America on ships about 1775 (Silver, 1927). It is native to Japan and possibly the eastern mainland of Asia.

The Norway rat is a moderately large, robust, grayish or brownish rodent with coarse fur and a long, sparsely haired, scaly tail. The tail is shorter than the combined length (approximately 80 percent) of the head and body. The underparts and feet are grayish to whitish.

Norway rats may be found wherever food and shelter are abundant. They are found in towns, cities, and rural areas. They may be found in barns, fields, ditches, corn cribs, and dumps. Unlike the black rat, they often burrow in the ground.

In the early 1930s, the Komareks recorded this species commonly around buildings and occasionally in rock fences bordering corn fields. However, they recorded one individual five miles from the nearest habitation along Eagle Rock Creek (3,800 feet). Due to a more limited food supply than in pre-park days, Norway rats have become less abundant in the park.

Individuals have been recorded at Gatlinburg (1,300 feet), Big Creek (1,700 feet), Greenbrier Cove (1,750 feet), and Elkmont (2,500 feet). In July, 1957, a half-grown individual was taken near a garbage can along the Clingmans Dome Road at an elevation of 6,000 feet (Stupka, 1957).

Norway rats often occur in colonies. They are mainly nocturnal and are active all year. They are aggressive and often drive out black rats as well as native rats and mice. They are omnivorous and feed on grain, green vegetation, meat, eggs, nestling birds, insects, fruit, and garbage. An adult rat will eat one-third of its weight in food every 24 hours.

Although this non-native rat harbors and carries diseases of humans and livestock and destroys large quantities of grain, fruits, and vegetables, it has one redeeming feature. The common laboratory, or white, rat is an albino strain of Norway rat. It has proven extremely valuable in many fields of biological and medical research.

If food and shelter are abundant, Norway rats may breed all year. Litters range in size from six to 22 young, but usually average seven to nine. A single female may give birth to as many as 12 litters in a year. Most Norway rats survive less than one year.

HOUSE MOUSE
Mus musculus

Tennessee - North Carolina — 1, 2

Total Length : 5 3/4 – 7 1/2 in (150 – 185 mm)
Tail : 2 4/5 – 4 in (74 – 100 mm)
Weight : 1/2 – 1 oz (14 – 28 g)

The house mouse is the only non-native (exotic) mouse occurring in the park. It is native to Eurasia and is thought to have arrived in the United States as a stowaway aboard transatlantic ships about the time of the American Revolution.

This is a small brownish-gray mouse with a long, slender, tapering, indistinctly bicolored tail. The tail is sparsely haired and scaly. The belly is grayish.

House mice are commonly found in and around human habitations, but in some areas they are also a common species in cultivated fields. The Komareks found them most frequently around cabins and barns. Like the two previous species, the house mouse is probably less common now than it was before the establishment of the park due to a more limited supply of food and shelter.

In the park, house mice have been recorded up to 2,700 feet. Localities include near park headquarters (1,500 feet), Greenbrier Cove (2,000 feet), Cades Cove (1,750 feet), Forney Creek, Elkmont (2,500 feet), and near Low Gap (2,700 feet).

Although house mice tend to be nocturnal, they may be active at any hour during all seasons. They are omnivorous and feed on grains, seeds, green vegetation, insects, and other invertebrates.

The familiar white, or laboratory, mouse widely used for research is an albino strain of the house mouse. Thus, this species has made valuable contributions to medical science and to human society.

In some areas, the house mouse breeds throughout the year. Litters may consist of as many as twelve young, although four to seven is average. Most individuals live less than two years.

———

JUMPING MICE
Family Zapodidae

Jumping mice can easily be distinguished from all other mice in Great Smoky Mountains National Park by their long hind legs, large hind feet, and a tail that is considerably longer than the body. In addition, the deep orange or yellow upper incisors are deeply grooved on their anterior surface.

Two members of this family — the meadow jumping mouse and the woodland jumping mouse —— occur in the park.

MEADOW JUMPING MOUSE
Zapus hudsonius

Tennessee - North Carolina — 1, 2

Total Length : 7 1/4 – 8 3/4 in (185 – 225 mm)
Tail : 4 1/4 – 5 3/4 in (110 – 150 mm)
Weight : 1/2 – 1 oz (12 – 28 g)

The upper parts of the medium-sized, long-tailed meadow jumping mouse are brownish-yellow mixed with black middorsally to form a dark stripe from the face to the base of the tail. The sides are dark yellowish-brown, and the underparts are white. The small, dark ears have a narrow, pale edge.

As its name implies, this species is found in open, grassy areas such as wet meadows, abandoned grassy fields, and forest glades, oftentimes near streams. The scarcity of such areas within the park and the fact that this species is near the southern limit of its range probably account for the fact that this is one of the rarest mice in Great Smoky Mountains National Park. As ecological succession progresses towards a more forested condition, it is unlikely that the meadow jumping mouse will ever become abundant in the park.

Prior to 1991, the meadow jumping mouse had been recorded on four occasions from only three areas in the park. On November 7, 1935, several hibernating individuals were dug out of a loose clay bank along Noland Creek (approximately 2,900 feet). Each was located in a separate compartment lined with dry leaves, approximately 18 inches below ground level. On February 7, 1941, near Deep Creek (1,750 feet), a single hibernating mouse was found four to six inches below the surface of a clean road fill. Both localities are in Swain County, North Carolina. The first recorded specimen from the Tennessee side of the park was taken by the author and his wife on August 3, 1964, approximately 450 feet northeast of Cosby Creek near the Cosby Ranger Station, at an elevation of 1,720 feet (Linzey and Linzey, 1966). It was found in an area of high weeds completely surrounded by deciduous woodlands. In 1984, a second individual was recorded in nearly the same location near the Cosby entrance to the park (Ambrose, 1986). In 1991, 12 individuals were taken along the Foothills Parkway at Cove Creek (1,430 feet) (Harvey, 1991).

Meadow jumping mice are mainly nocturnal and are active only during the warmer months. They hibernate during the colder winter months. Hibernation is usually in a lined burrow (hibernaculum) below the frost line. When hibernating, jumping mice normally curl into a ball with their nose and feet on their abdomen and their tail curled around their body.

Seeds are the primary food, but berries, nuts, fruits, and insects are also eaten. Breeding begins shortly after emerging from hibernation with most litters being produced during June and again in August. Litters may range from three to seven. Several individuals have lived at least two years in the wild.

WOODLAND JUMPING MOUSE
Napaeozapus insignis

Tennessee - North Carolina — 1, 2, 3, 4, 5, 6

Total Length : 8 1/4 – 9 3/4 in (210 – 250 mm)
Tail : 4 4/5 – 5 4/5 in (125 – 150 mm)
Weight : 3/4 – 1 oz (21 – 28 g)

The medium-sized woodland jumping mouse has bright orange-brown sides, a dark median dorsal band, and white underparts. The long, bicolored tail usually ends in a white tip, unlike the dark tip of the meadow jumping mouse.

the neck are rusty-yellow. The long, bushy tail has a median black stripe and a black tip.

The gray fox is a common inhabitant of the lower elevations in the park. The highest recorded occurrence has been Newfound Gap. Representative localities include park headquarters, Big Creek, Cades Cove (1,800 to 2,000 feet), Cooper Creek, Pilot Ridge, Smokemont, and Elkmont (2,500 feet).

Unlike the red fox, this species prefers forested areas; thus, this is the common fox throughout the deciduous forests of the eastern and southern United States. Heavily wooded swamps as well as rough, hilly terrain near streams and lakes provide ideal habitat.

The gray fox is primarily nocturnal and is active during all seasons. Dens may be located in slab and scrap piles around abandoned sawmills, in hollow logs, under rocks, and in ground burrows. Den sites are usually located in dense cover.

The gray fox is a tree-climbing fox. It often seeks refuge in a tree when being pursued. It may leap upon limbs of low trees and hop from branch to branch as it ascends, or it may hug the trunk with its forelimbs and force itself upward with its hind limbs.

This fox is omnivorous. It is an opportunistic feeder and depends on seasonal food availability. Major foods consist of small mammals such as rabbits and rodents, insects, birds and other vertebrates, nuts, and fruits. Examination of the stomach contents of an individual found near Smokemont in August, 1934, revealed grasshoppers, beetles, pokeweed seeds, and a spider. The stomach of a young male found near Smokemont on October 30, 1939, contained several persimmon seeds, an acorn, a maple seed, and the fur of a small mammal. An individual found between Townsend and the park boundary on September 13, 1950, contained 70 percent invertebrates and 30 percent vegetation (Pfitzer, 1950). The stomach of another fox found near Smokemont in late September, 1950, contained 95 percent camel crickets and 5 percent other insects and centipedes (Pfitzer, 1950). Other food items found in the stomachs of various individuals include acorns, maple seeds, persimmons, and various small mammals.

Young gray foxes are usually born in March or April. Average litters consist of four pups. The young foxes remain with the female until fall at which time they disperse. Wild gray foxes probably live for several years.

BEARS

Family Ursidae

Bears are the largest living carnivores. The big brown bear may weigh more than 1,500 pounds (675 kg). Bears have small ears and eyes and short tails. They walk in the same manner as does man by placing the entire lower surface of each foot on the ground.

Four kinds of bears (black, grizzly, big brown, and polar) occur in the United States, but only the black bear inhabits the Great Smoky Mountains National Park.

BLACK BEAR
Ursus americanus
Tennessee - North Carolina — 1, 2, 3, 4, 5, 6

Total Length : 54 – 72 in (1,370 – 1,830 mm)
Tail : 4 – 5 in (100 – 125 mm)
Height at Shoulder : 24 – 36 in (600 – 900 mm)
Weight : 150 – 400 lbs (68 – 180 kg)

The black bear is currently the park's largest native mammal and, for the visitor, its most popular animal. These large carnivores are usually glossy black with a brown muzzle. A small, white patch is often present on the chest. The legs are short and stout, and the short tail is almost concealed in the long shaggy fur. An adult female with four white feet was captured in the Sugarlands area. Other sightings of white-footed bears have been reported from the same area.

Bear population numbers fluctuate irregularly due to periodic years of poor mast (acorns and hickory nuts) production. Currently, about 400 to 600 black bears inhabit the park. Their average age is 4 1/2 years (McLean,

WEASELS, SKUNKS, AND OTHER MUSTELIDS
Family Mustelidae

The family Mustelidae contains a large and varied group of predatory mammals including the fisher, mink, weasels, ferrets, martens, wolverines, badgers, skunks, and otters. Most have long slender bodies, short legs, short rounded ears, and anal scent glands. Most members of this family are nocturnal and are active all year.

FISHER [Extirpated?]
Martes pennanti

Tennessee — (?)

Total Length : 32 – 40 in (810 – 1,040 mm)
Tail : 13 – 16 in (330 – 400 mm)
Weight : 3 – 12 lbs (1.3 – 5.4 kg)

The fisher is a large dark brown to nearly black weasel-like animal with a bushy, tapering tail. White-tipped hairs give the animal a frosted appearance.

Concerning its possible presence in the park, Linzey and Linzey (1971) stated:

"It is uncertain whether the Fisher ever occurred in the area encompassed by the Park. Miller and Kellogg (1955) noted that this animal was found as far south as North Carolina. This range was extended by Parmalee (1960), who found the jawbone of a Fisher in Bartow County, Georgia.

"Audubon and Bachman (1846) stated: 'We have seen several skins procured in east Tennessee . . . . ' During a journey of several hundred miles through the mountains of Tennessee and North Carolina during the summer of 1887, Merriam (1888) found no trace of the Fisher, which he refers to as the 'Pekan'."

The fisher was successfully restocked in West Virginia in 1969. The animals are reproducing and several have been observed in western Virginia. The possibility of reintroducing the fisher to the Great Smoky Mountains National Park has been discussed. After examining various aspects of the animal's biology and its potential effects on other species, the decision was made not to proceed at the present time.

LONG-TAILED WEASEL
Mustela frenata

Tennessee - North Carolina — 1, 2, 3, 4, 5, 6

Total Length : 13 – 17 in (330 – 445 mm)
Tail : 4 – 6 in (100 – 150 mm)
Weight : 3 – 10 oz (85 – 280 g)

The fairly large long-tailed weasel has a long tail with a distinct black tip. During the summer, the long-tailed weasel is dark brown above and buff or yellowish-white below. During the winter, the dorsal pelage is buff-brown.

The long-tailed weasel is found in a wide variety of habitats including farmland, woodlands, and swamps. Hedgerows and brushy fields often provide good habitat. Areas near water seem to be preferred.

The long-tailed weasel is a fairly common resident of Great Smoky Mountains National Park and has been found at all elevations. Individuals have been observed along Little River (1,400 feet), Sugarlands (1,500 to 1,600 feet), Cataloochee, Noisy Creek, along the Newfound Gap Road (2,900 feet, 4,000 feet), Greenbrier Cove (3,500 feet), Greenbrier Pinnacle (4,500 feet), and Mount LeConte (6,300 feet; 6,593 feet).

These solitary animals may be active at any hour during all seasons. They are intensely active and alert and possess well developed senses of hearing, sight, and smell. They are extremely quick in their movements, and they are tireless hunters. Dens may be in a hollow stump, in sawmill slab piles, in an unused underground burrow, in a rock pile, or even in a building such as a barn.

These carnivorous animals feed primarily on mice, rats, shrews, and moles. Their diet may also occasionally include rabbits, squirrels, birds, snakes, lizards, insects, and earthworms. In June, 1944, a long-tailed weasel was seen on Mount LeConte carrying a deermouse in its mouth.

Breeding usually occurs in July and August with the young being born in April. The long gestation is caused by delayed implantation of the embryos in the uterus. Litters may consist of four to nine young. In late April, 1961, Herrick Brown discovered a nest of this species in a building near LeConte Lodge. The nest contained five or six young, each about four inches in length with their eyes not yet open. The young are fully grown at 10 weeks. Both parents assist in bringing food to the young and caring for them. Wild individuals are known to have lived for three years.

When frightened or angered, the eastern spotted skunk may engage in several unique behaviors that may serve as either a bluff or a warning prior to the discharge of the scent. It may stamp or pat its front feet in rapid succession on the floor or ground. It can also do a "handstand" on its front feet. The skunk upends itself, holds its tail in the air, and may walk up to several yards in this manner.

The eastern spotted skunk is omnivorous. It feeds primarily on small mammals, fruits, insects, birds, lizards, snakes, and carrion. The stomach of a specimen found near park headquarters in November, 1950, contained the remains of a northern spring peeper (*Hyla crucifer*), a short-tailed shrew, one katydid, one camel cricket, several clover leaves, and miscellaneous arthropod remains (Pfitzer, 1950).

Litters of two to six young are usually born during May or June. Delayed implantation occurs and greatly prolongs gestation. The young are weaned at about eight weeks. Life expectancy in the wild is unknown, although a captive skunk lived almost 10 years.

STRIPED SKUNK
Mephitis mephitis

Tennessee - North Carolina — 1, 2, 3, 4, 5
Total Length : 21 – 29 in (550 – 750 mm)
Tail : 7 – 12 in (175 – 300 mm)
Weight : 3 – 10 lbs (1.3 – 4.5 kg)

The striped skunk is the larger and more common of the two skunks inhabiting the park. This short-legged, housecat-sized mammal is black with a narrow white stripe running up the middle of the forehead and a broad white area on the nape of the neck that usually divides into a V at about the shoulders. The resulting two white stripes may continue to the base of the bushy tail. The white stripes show considerable variation. In some animals, they are broad and well defined; in others, they are absent. The striped skunk has a relatively small head with short-rounded ears, small eyes, and a pointed muzzle. Two large musk glands are located at the base of the tail.

These animals inhabit old fields and brushy areas as well as sparsely wooded regions. Agricultural areas with their mix of open cropland and brushy or wooded edges provide ideal habitat. Komarek and Komarek (1938) noted that the striped skunk was generally distributed throughout the mountains but was probably more commonly associated with the open fields and cut-over woodlands of the lower elevations.

In the park, striped skunks have been recorded at elevations up to 5,200 feet. Representative localities include Cades Cove (1,800 feet), Sugarlands (2,000 feet), Elkmont (2,000 feet), Smokemont, Greenbrier Cove (2,700 to 3,000 feet), Walnut Bottom, Mingus and Cooper Creek Divide (3,500 feet), Pin Oak Gap, Spence Field (5,000 feet), Newfound Gap (5,045 feet), and Indian Gap (5,200 feet).

Striped skunks are primarily solitary, nocturnal mammals. They spend the day in underground burrows, beneath abandoned buildings, in hollow logs, or in wood piles. Although active individuals have been observed in the park during every month, they may become dormant for prolonged periods during severe winter weather. Unlike the eastern spotted skunk, they are not good climbers.

Striped skunks are omnivorous and feed primarily on small rodents, eggs, insects and their larvae, berries, and carrion. Birds and reptiles may be taken occasionally. In February, 1935, a skunk was observed on Messer Fork following a plow and eating grubs (Fleetwood, 1934-1935). On November 26, 1937, Stupka examined the stomach of an individual found near Elkmont and noted the seeds and pulp of persimmon, insect remains (grasshopper, Hemiptera, and larvae), and the feathers of a small bird.

Litters of four to seven young are produced in spring. The young usually remain with the mother until late summer when they disperse. In the wild, striped skunks may live for five to six years.

Because of its well-known and effective defense mechanism, the striped skunk is not molested by many animals. Palmer (1954) stated, however, that "practically every Horned Owl in the skunk's range smells of skunk — one of its staple foods." On two occasions in the park, Stupka noted great horned owls which had a strong odor of skunk about them.

NORTHERN RIVER OTTER
(Extirpated; Reintroduced)
Lutra canadensis

Tennessee - North Carolina — 1, 2, 3, 4

Total Length : 37 – 49 in (950 – 1,250 mm)
Tail : 12 – 19 in (300 – 475 mm)
Weight : 10 – 25 lbs (4.5 – 11.5 kg)

The northern river otter is a slender, long-bodied, short-legged mammal with a broad, flat head and a muscular body. The snout is

Varner. The bat was compared to the photograph of a seminole bat in Harvey (1992) and was almost identical in appearance (Stiver, personal communication, October, 1993). It was subsequently released in the park headquarters area. This species is included in this section 1) because it was not actually taken in the park and 2) because no specimen exists for positive identification.

EVENING BAT
Nycticeius humeralis

Hall (1981) showed the range of this bat covering the entire southeastern United States. It has been called the "third commonest species" in North Carolina (Brimley, 1944-1946). Paul and Quay (1963) reported one individual from the Toxaway River Gorge. Kellogg (1939) recorded specimens from counties in Tennessee west of the mountains.

TOWNSEND'S (WESTERN) BIG-EARED BAT
Plecotus townsendii

The park lies just south of the range of this species as presented by Hall (1981). Neither Kellogg (1939) nor Smith, Funderburg, and Quay (1960) reported any specimens from Tennessee and North Carolina, respectively. Recently, however, this species has been recorded from one site in western North Carolina (Harvey, 1992).

PORCUPINE
Erethizon dorsatum

The nearest records of this species are from Spruce Knob in West Virginia, although Hall (1981) indicated that its range may extend through the mountains as far south as the Smokies. Jawbones of porcupines have been recovered from archaeological sites west of Chattanooga in Marion County, Tennessee (Parmalee and Guilday, 1966).

LEAST WEASEL
Mustela nivalis

This weasel has been taken in western North Carolina on four occasions. On April 17, 1916, the first specimen was reported from Marshall, Madison County, approximately 25 miles northeast of the park (Church, 1925). The second weasel was taken from a cat at Balsam Gap (3,400 feet), Jackson County, on July 24, 1959 (Stupka, 1960a). This locality is approximately 10 miles southeast of the park. Edwards (1963) took a third individual near Asheville, 25 miles east of the park. A fourth North Carolina specimen was recorded on November 17, 1965, four miles northeast of Hendersonville, Henderson County, at an elevation of 2,200 feet (Barkalow, 1967). This locality is within 10 miles of the South Carolina border and represents the southernmost limit of the species. The lone Tennessee record of the least weasel is a specimen taken on Roan Mountain (4,800 feet), Carter County, on September 25, 1962 (Tuttle, 1968). This locality is approximately 70 miles northeast of the Great Smoky Mountains National Park.

Eptesicus fuscus fuscus	Big Brown Bat
Lasiurus borealis	Eastern Red Bat
Lasiurus cinereus	Hoary Bat
Plecotus rafinesquii	Rafinesque's (Eastern) Big-eared Bat

Family LEPORIDAE
Sylvilagus floridanus floridanus	Eastern Cottontail
Sylvilagus obscurus	Appalachian Cottontail

Family SCIURIDAE
Tamias striatus	Eastern Chipmunk
Marmota monax	Woodchuck
Sciurus carolinensis	Eastern Gray Squirrel
Sciurus niger	Eastern Fox Squirrel
Tamiasciurus hudsonicus	Red Squirrel
Glaucomys volans volans	Southern Flying Squirrel
Glaucomys sabrinus	Northern Flying Squirrel

Family CASTORIDAE
Castor canadensis	American Beaver

Family MURIDAE
Oryzomys palustris palustris	Marsh Rice Rat
Reithrodontomys humulis	Eastern Harvest Mouse
Peromyscus leucopus leucopus	White-footed Mouse
Peromyscus maniculatus maniculatus	Deermouse
Peromyscus gossypinus gossypinus	Cotton Mouse
Ochrotomys nuttalli	Golden Mouse
Sigmodon hispidus hispidus	Hispid Cotton Rat
Neotoma magister	Allegheny Woodrat
Synaptomys cooperi stonei	Southern Bog Lemming
Clethrionomys gapperi gapperi	Southern Red-backed Vole
Microtus pennsylvanicus pennsylvanicus	Meadow Vole
Microtus chrotorrhinus	Rock Vole
Microtus pinetorum	Woodland Vole
Ondatra zibethicus	Common Muskrat
Rattus norvegicus norvegicus	Norway Rat
Rattus rattus	Black Rat
Mus musculus	House Mouse

Family ZAPODIDAE
    Zapus hudsonius   Meadow Jumping Mouse
    Napaeozapus insignis   Woodland Jumping Mouse

Family CANIDAE
    Canis latrans   Coyote
    *Canis lupus lycaon   Gray Wolf
    Canis rufus rufus   Red Wolf
    Vulpes vulpes   Red Fox
    Urocyon cinereoargenteus cinereoargenteus   Gray Fox

Family URSIDAE
    Ursus americanus americanus   Black Bear

Family PROCYONIDAE
    Procyon lotor lotor   Raccoon

Family MUSTELIDAE
    *Martes pennanti   Fisher
    Mustela frenata   Long-tailed Weasel
    Mustela vison   Mink
    Spilogale putorius   Eastern Spotted Skunk
    Mephitis mephitis   Striped Skunk
    Lutra canadensis   Northern River Otter

Family FELIDAE
    Felis concolor   Mountain Lion
    Lynx rufus   Bobcat

Family SUIDAE
    Sus scrofa   Wild Hog

Family CERVIDAE
    *Cervus elaphus   American Elk (Wapiti)
    Odocoileus virginianus   White-tailed Deer

Family BOVIDAE
    *Bison bison bison   American Bison

TOWNSEND LIBER (336 m)
Town in Tuckaleechee Cove, 3 miles north of park boundary (Tennessee)

TOWNSEND Y LIBER (351 m)
Junction of Little River and Middle Prong of Little River (Tennessee)

TREMONT L336 ft (397 m)
On Middle Prong of Little River near junction with Lynn Camp Prong (Tennessee)

TRILLIUM GAP 4,310 ft (1,314 m)
Between Mount LeConte and Brushy Mountain [Tennessee]

TROUT BRANCH approximately 3,630 ft (Creek) (1,106 m)
Tributary of West Prong of Little Pigeon River, along Newfound Gap Road above the Loop Tunnel (Tennessee)

TWENTYMILE CREEK 1,513 - 4,160 ft (461 -1,268 m)
Flows into Cheoah Lake on park boundary west of Fontana Dam (North Carolina)

WALKER CREEK approximately 3,280 - 4,675 ft (1,095 - 1,425 m)
Tributary of Hazel Creek (North Carolina)

WALKER PRONG approximately 4,430 ft (South) (1,350 m)
Tributary of West Prong of Little Pigeon River (Tennessee)

WARDEN BRANCH 3,030 ft (923 m)
On Big Creek in northeastern part of park (North Carolina)

WEARCOVE 1,454 ft (443 m)
On park boundary north of Cove Mountain (Tennessee)

WEST PRONG OF LITTLE PIGEON RIVER (same as West Fork of Little Pigeon River)
approximately 1,280 - 4,590 ft (390 - 1,399 m)
Near Gatlinburg and flows through Gatlinburg, Tennessee

WET BOTTOM approximately 2,340 ft

WITIT GAP

Photographers Credits

Robert H. Baker: 50
Roger W. Barbour: 11, 11, 12, 20, 21, 21, 22, 23, 24, 25 (upper), 26, 81
Christina M. Bird: 88
Richard E. Bird: 30, 32, 84
Joseph A. Chapman: 31
Kenneth L. Crowell: 54
L. Elliott: 52, 63
Thomas W. French: 10
General Biological Supply Company: 9
Daisy Gibbs: 33
Great Smoky Mountains National Park: 35, 37, 69, 71, 73, 75, 78, 82, 90, 93, 96
George Harrison, United States Fish and Wildlife Service: 65
Graham C. Hickman: 18
Ken L. Jenkins: front cover, 92
Donald W. Linzey: 13
John R. MacGregor: 16, 25 (lower), 27, 46, 53, 59, 60, 62, 83
Lawrence L. Master: 80
David Mech, United States Fish and Wildlife Service: 67
Jon Nickle, United States Fish and Wildlife Service: 36
Ron Singer, United States Fish and Wildlife Service: 85
Tom Smylie, United States Fish and Wildlife Service: 41
E. J. Taylor: 58
Ken Taylor, North Carolina Wildlife Resources Commission: 40
Tennessee Wildlife Resource Agency: 38, 70
R. Town, United States Fish and Wildlife Service: 57
R. Wayne VanDevender: 14, 15, 17, 43, 44, 45, 47, 49, 51, 55, 56
Susan L. Woodward: 7, 95, 99

Index

Abrams Branch, 39
Abrams Creek, 2, 42, 57, 86, 87
Abrams Creek Ranger Station, 51
Alarka Creek, 42
Alum Cave Bluffs, 78
Alum Cave Parking Area, 31, 64
Alum Cave Trail, 17
American Chestnut; *see* Chestnut, American
Andrews Bald, 10, 54
Appalachian Mountains, 2, 3
Appalachian Trail, 18, 23, 64, 71
Asheville, NC, 67, 101, 103

Balsam; *see* Fir
Bat, 1, 2, **19-28**
  Big Brown, **25**, 118
  Big-eared; *see* Rafinesque's
  Eastern Pipistrelle, **24**, 117
  Eastern Small-footed Myotis, **22-23**, 117
  Evening, **102**
  Gray Myotis, **101**
  Hoary, 19, **26-27**, 118
  Indiana, **21-22**, 117
  Little Brown Myotis, **20-21**
  Northern Myotis, **21**
  Rafinesque's (Eastern) Big-eared, **27-28**, 118
  Red, Eastern, 19, 20, **25-26**, 118
  Seminole, **101**
  Silver-haired, 19, **23**, 117
  Social; *see* Indiana
  Southeastern Myotis, **101**
  Townsend's (Western) Big-eared, **102**
Bear,
  Big Brown, 73
  Black, 1, 4, 5, 35, 66, 70, **73-77**, 94, 98, 119
  Grizzly, 73
  Polar, 73

Beaver, 1, 2, **41-42**
Becks Bald, 71
Beech Flats Prong, 12
Big Cove, 35
Big Creek, 39, 49, 51, 60, 64, 68, 72, 82, 83, 86, 89, 97
Bird, 71, 72, 79, 81, 84, 85, 91
  Duck, 82
  Grouse, 69, 91
  Hawk, 79, 82
  Nuthatch, Red-breasted, 37
  Owl, 8, 9, 15, 30, 47, 64, 79, 82, 85, 91
  Robin, 91
  Wild Turkey, 90
Bison, American, 1, **99-100**, 119
Bison bison, **99-100**, 119
Blanket Mountain, 17, 39, 40
Blarina brevicauda, **14-15**, 117
Blowhole Cave, 21, 22, 24, 25, 28
Bobcat, 9, 10, 15, 33, 35, 36, 46, 55, 64, 76, 79, 88, **90-91**, 94, 98, 119
Bog Lemming; *see* Mouse, Southern Bog Lemming
Bote Mountain, 17, 52
Boulevard Trail, The, 71
Bovidae, **99-100**, 119
Bradley Fork, 36, 54, 57
Bryson City, NC, 42
Bryson Place, 86
Buck Fork, 10, 54, 64
Buck Prong, 10, 52, 54
Buena Vista, 39
Buffalo; *see* Bison
Bull Cave, 21, 22, 24
Bullhead Trail, 64

Cades Cove, 2, 15, 17, 23, 24, 25, 26, 28, 33, 39, 42, 48, 51, 55, 57, 61, 66, 68, 69, 72, 75, 76, 78, 82,

85, 89, 90, 92, 97
Calderwood, NC, 92
Caldwell Fork, 82
Caney Creek, 10, 13
Canidae, **65-72**, 119
Canis
 latrans, **65-66**, 119
 lupus, **67-68**, 119
 rufus, **69-70**, 119
Castor canadensis, **41-42**, 118
Castoridae, **41-42**, 118
Cat, Domestic, 18, 88
Cataloochee, 17, 21, 25, 51, 55, 56, 66, 75, 78, 81,
 82, 83, 86, 97
Cataloochee Mountains, 67
Catamount; *see* Mountain Lion
Cervidae, **95-98**, 119
Cervus elaphus, **95-96**, 119
Chambers Creek, 51, 52, 86
Chapman Prong, 17, 52
Charlies Bunion, 18
Cherokee, NC, 3
Cherokee Indian Reservation, 51, 53, 66
Cherokee Orchard, 49, 55
Chestnut, American, 4, 5, 35, 39
Chilhowee Mountains, 74
Chimneys Campground (*see* Chimneys Picnic
 Area)
Chimneys Parking Overlook, 76
Chimneys Picnic Area, 54, 64, 67, 83, 91
Chipmunk, Eastern, 1, 2, **32-33**, 118
Civet; *see* Skunk, Spotted
Clethrionomys gapperi, **52-53**, 118
Cliff Branch, 82, 83, 91
Clingmans Dome, 2, 10, 13, 17, 30, 33, 53, 91
Clingmans Dome Road 60, 76, 91
Collins Creek, 97
Collins Gap, 53
Condylura cristata, **18**, 117
Cooper Creek, 72
Cosby, 2, 5, 15, 17, 24, 25, 26, 33, 45, 46, 48, 49,
 52, 55, 57, 63, 64, 71, 97
Cosby Campground, 76
Cosby Creek, 46, 63, 64
Cosby Ranger Station, 63
Couches Creek, 49, 91

Cottontail, 71
 Appalachian, 29, **31**, 118
 Eastern, 29, **30**, 31, 118
 New England, 31
Cougar; *see* Mountain Lion
Cove Creek, 10, 13, 15, 45, 49, 51, 55
Coyote, 1, **65-66**, 68, 69, 94, 119
Cryptotis parva, **15**, 117

Dalton Ridge, 66
Deep Creek, 2, 18, 33, 39, 42, 49, 55, 57, 63, 86, 97
Deep Creek Ranger Station, 23
Deer, White-tailed, 1, 4, 66, 69, 70, 76, 90, 95,
 96-98, 119
Deermouse, 81
Didelphidae, **7**, 117
Didelphis virginiana, **7-8**, 117
Dog, 79, 98
Double Springs Gap, 66
Dry Sluice Gap, 10
Dudley Creek, 71

Eagle Creek, 27, 36, 42, 66, 86
Eagle Creek Mines, 28
Eagle Rock Creek, 52, 54, 59, 64
Elk, American, 1, **95-96**, 119
Elkmont, 2, 15, 17, 21, 31, 33, 49, 55, 56, 57, 58, 60,
 61, 64, 66, 68, 72, 74, 78, 79, 85, 87
Eptesicus fuscus, **25**, 118
Erethizon dorsatum, **102**

Felidae, **88-91**, 119
Felis concolor, **88-90**, 119
Fighting Creek, 15, 48, 49, 97
Fighting Creek Gap, 36, 66
Fir, 2, 4, 33, 34, 37, 40, 64, 97
Fish, 79, 82, 87
 Hogsucker, Northern, 87
 Stoneroller Minnow, 87
 Sucker, White, 87
 Trout, 83
Fish Camp Prong, 15
Fisher, 1, **80**, 119
Flat Creek, 10
Fontana Dam, 26
Fontana Lake (Fontana Reservoir), 42, 51, 92, 97

Fontana Village, 89
Foothills Parkway, 8, 10, 13, 15, 21, 24, 33, 36, 39, 45, 51, 63
Forney Creek, 28, 53, 56, 57, 61, 71, 74, 83, 86
Forney Ridge, 10, 34, 64, 78
Fort Harry Cliffs, 13, 54
Fox, 1, 4, 9, 15, 33, 35, 58, 66, 79, 82, 91
  Gray, 65, **71-72**, 119
  Red, 65, **70-71**, 119
French Broad River, 86
Frog, 58, 87
  Northern Spring Peeper, 84
  Wood, 8, 79

Gatlinburg, 2, 15, 27, 48, 51, 57, 60, 67, 76, 101
Glaucomys,
  sabrinus, **40**, 118
  volans, **38-39**, 118
Gnatty Branch, 51
Grassy Patch, 54, 56, 64
Greenbrier, 10, 12, 13, 17, 23, 25, 28, 39, 44, 48, 50, 51, 56, 78, 82, 86, 89, 90, 97
Greenbrier Cove, 15, 21, 23, 24, 26, 49, 52, 54, 55, 57, 58, 60, 61, 71, 81, 83, 85
Greenbrier Pinnacle, 81
Gregory Bald, 17, 66, 86, 92
Gregory Ridge Trail, 98
Gregory's Cave, 24, 28
Groundhog; *see* Woodchuck
Gum Stand, 51

Happy Valley Ranger Station, 51
Hare, Varying, 29
Hawk, 9, 30, 33, 58
Hazel Creek, 36, 42, 66, 78, 87, 97, 98
Heintooga 91, 97
Hog, Wild, 1, 4, 76, **92-94**, 98, 119

Indian Camp Creek, 54
Indian Creek, 55, 57
Indian Gap, 10, 18, 23, 40, 53, 54, 56, 64, 71, 78, 85, 91

Jakes Creek, 91
Jonas Creek, 53, 56

Jumping Mouse,
  Meadow, 2, **62-63**, 119
  Woodland, 2, 62, **63-64**, 91, 119

Kanati Fork, 52, 54, 56
Kephart Prong, 26, 64
Kephart Prong Hatchery, 18
King Hollow Branch, 13, 45, 49, 55, 64

Lasionycteris noctivagans, **23**, 117
Lasiurus,
  borealis, **25-26**, 118
  cinereus, **26-27**, 118
Laurel Branch, 44
Laurel Creek, 48, 66, 78
Laurel Falls, 66
LeConte Lodge, 25, 81
Leporidae, **29-31**
Lepus americanus, **29**
Little Pigeon River, 12
  Middle Prong, 12, 86
  West Prong, 12, 13, 52, 54, 86
Little River, 48, 49, 56, 58, 64, 66, 81, 82, 83, 86
Little River Road 18, 36, 51, 91
Lizard, 81, 84
Low Gap, 24, 31, 52, 61, 64
Lutra canadensis, **85-87**, 119
Lynx, 88
Lynx,
  rufus, **88**, 119
  canadensis, **88**

Maddron Bald Trail, 78, 82
Maples Ranch, 10
Marmota monax, **33-35**, 118
Marsupial, 7
Martes pennanti, **80**, 119
Meigs Creek, 23
Mephitis mephitis, **84-85**
Messer Fork, 85
Metcalf Bottoms, 17, 58, 71, 76, 78, 82
Microtus,
  chrotorrhinus, **54-55**, 91, 118
  pennsylvanicus, **53-54**, 118
  pinetorum, **55-56**, 118
Mill Creek, 36, 64

Mingus and Cooper Creek Divide, 85
Mingus Mill Creek, 54
Mink, 1, 58, 80, **82-83**, 119
Miry Ridge Trail, 17, 18
Mole, 1, **16-18**, 81
  Eastern, **16-17**, 81, 117
  Hairy-tailed, **17-18**, 117
  Star-nosed, **18**, 117
Mountain Lion, 4, 76, **88-90**, 119
Mount Buckley, 17
Mount Cammerer, 29, 64
Mount Collins, 10, 17, 53
Mount Guyot, 10, 29, 33, 45, 53
Mount Kephart, 10, 17, 53, 54
Mount LeConte, 2, 30, 59, 68, 71, 78, 81, 82, 91
Mount Sterling, 51, 78, 86
Mount Sterling Creek, 82
Mouse, 1, 2, 14, 71, 81, 82
  Cotton, **47-48**, 118
  Deer, **45-46**, 81, 91, 118
  Eastern Harvest, 2, 4, 43, **44-45**, 118
  Golden, 2, **49-50**, 118
  House, **60-61**
  Meadow Vole, **53-54**, 118
  Meadow Jumping, 2, **62-63**, 119
  Rock Vole, 2, 3, **54-55**, 91, 118
  Southern Bog Lemming, **56-57**, 118
  Southern Red-backed Vole, **52-53**, 118
  White-footed, 5, 45, **46-47**, 48, 118
  Woodland Jumping, 2, 62, **63-64**, 91, 119
  Woodland Vole, **55-56**, 118
Muridae, **43-61**, 118
Mus musculus, **60-61**, 118
Muskrat, 2, 43, **57-58**, 82, 118
Mustela,
  frenata, **81-82**, 119
  nivalis, **102**
  vison, **82-83**, 119
Mustelidae, **80-87**, 102-103, 119
Myhr Cave, 21, 24, 26, 27
Myotis,
  Eastern Small-footed, **22-23**, 117
  Gray, **101**
  Indiana, **21-22**, 117
  Little Brown, **20-21**, 117
  Northern, **21**, 117

  Southeastern, **101**
Myotis,
  austroriparius, **101**
  grisescens, **101**
  leibii, **22-23**, 117
  lucifugus, **20-21**, 117
  septentrionalis, **21**, 117
  sodalis, **21-22**, 117

Napaeozapus insignis, **63-64**, 91, 119
Neotoma magister, **51-52**, 118
Newfound Gap, 2, 13, 17, 18, 23, 37, 40, 53, 54, 72, 85
Newfound Gap Road, 10, 13, 37, 52, 57, 64, 76, 81, 91
Newt Prong, 91
Noisy Creek, 81
Noland Creek, 42, 63, 86, 97
Noland Divide, 8
Nuthatch, Red-breasted, 37
Nycticeius humeralis, **102**

Ochrotomys nuttalli, **49-50**, 118
Oconaluftee River, 12, 42, 53, 54, 57, 82, 86
Oconaluftee Visitor Center, 17
Odocoileus virginianus, **96-98**, 119
Old Black Mountain, 10
Ondatra zibethicus, **57-58**, 118
Opossum, Virginia, 1, 4, **7-8**, 9, 117
Orter; *see* Otter, River,
Oryzomys palustris, **43-44**, 118
Otter, Northern River, 1, 4, 58, 80, **85-87**, 119
Owl, 9, 30
  Barred, 15
  Great Horned, 85, 91
  Screech, 8, 47, 64

Painter; *see* Mountain Lion
Palmer Branch, 66
Panther; *see* Mountain Lion
Parascalops breweri, **17-18**, 117
Park Headquarters, 10, 15, 17, 21, 22, 23, 25, 28, 36, 48, 58, 61, 64, 71, 72, 75, 83, 84, 90
Parson Branch, 66, 76
Pecks Corner, 54
Pekan; *see* Fisher
Peromyscus, 91

gossypinus, **47-48**, 118
leucopus, **46-47**, 118
maniculatus, **45-46**, 118
Pilkey Creek, 86
Pilot Ridge, 72
Pin Oak Gap, 85
Pine Knot Branch, 31
Pinnacle Creek, 42
Pinnacle Mountain, 91
Pipistrellus subflavus, **24**, 117
Pisgah Creek, 67
Pisgah Ridge, 67
Plecotus rafinesquii, **27-28**, 118
Porcupine, **102**
Porter's Flat, 23
Proctor, 36
Proctor Creek, 78
Procyon lotor, **78-79**, 119
Procyonidae, **78-79**, 119
Puma; *see* Mountain Lion

Rabbit, 1, 14, **29-31**, 66, 70, 72, 81, 82, 90, 91
Raccoon, 1, 4, 58, 70, **78-79**, 119
Rainbow Falls Trail, 17, 18, 57
Rat, 1, 81
  Allegheny Woodrat, **51-52**, 118
  Black, **58-59**, 60, 118
  Hispid Cotton, 4, **50-51**, 118
  Marsh Rice, 4, **43-44**, 118
  Norway, **59-60**, 118
Rattus,
  norvegicus, **59-60**, 118
  rattus, **58-59**, 118
Reithrodontomys humulis, **44-45**, 118
Roaring Fork, 48, 56
Rocky Spring Gap, 10
Rodent, 66, 72, 85, 90, 91
Round Bottom, 78
Russell Field, 97

Salamander, 79, 94
  Red-cheeked, 94
Saltpeter Cave, 21, 24
Scalopus aquaticus, **16-17**, 117
Schoolhouse Camp, 45
Sciuridae, **32-40**, 118

Sciurus,
  carolinensis, **35-36**, 91, 118
  niger, **36**, 118
Shrew, 1, 2, **8-15**, 81, 91, 117
  Short-tailed, 8, 9, **14-15**, 84, 117
  Least, 2, 4, **15**, 117
  Long-tailed, **12-13**
  Masked, **9-10**, 11, 117
  Water, 3, **11-12**, 117
  Pygmy, 1, 8, **13**, 117
  Smokey, **11**, 117
  Southeastern, **10**, 117
Shuckstack Tower, 36
Sigmodon hispidus, **50-51**, 118
Silers Bald, 53, 54, 56
Sinking Creek, 68
Sinks, The, 17, 48, 49, 51, 82
Skunk, 1, 9, 66, 80
  Spotted, 2, 15, **83-84**, 85, 119
  Striped, 83, **84-85**, 119
Smokemont, 2, 10, 18, 33, 39, 49, 54, 58, 64, 72, 85, 89, 91, 97
Smokemont Campground, 53
Snake, 8, 9, 30, 33, 58, 71, 79, 81, 82, 84
  Black Rat, 15, 30, 33, 39
  Copperhead, 15, 17, 55, 56
  Corn, 18, 56
  Timber Rattlesnake, 30, 33, 35, 36, 39, 46, 47, 53, 55, 64, 82
Snake Den Mountain, 39
Sorex, 91
  cinereus, **9-10**, 117
  dispar, **12-13**, 117
  fumeus, **11**, 117
  hoyi, **13**, 117
  longirostris, **10**, 117
  palustris, **11-12**, 117
Soricidae, **8-15**, 117
Spence Field, 17, 53, 54, 55, 56, 71, 85, 89
Spilogale putorius, **83-84**, 119
Spruce, 2, 33, 34, 37, 40, 56, 64, 74, 97
Spruce Knob, WV, 102
Squirrel, 1, 4, 5, 81
  Eastern Fox, 2, **36**, 118
  Eastern Gray, 32, **35-36**, 91, 118
  Ground; *see* Chipmunk

Northern Flying, 2, 3, 38, **40**, 118
 Red, 2, 3, 32, **37-38**, 118
 Southern Flying, 32, **38-39**, 40, 118
Straight Fork, 71
Sugar Fork Mine, 28
Sugarlands, 2, 17, 21, 24, 26, 28, 51, 66, 67, 73, 76,
 78, 81, 82, 83, 85, 86
Suidae, **92-94**, 119
Sus scrofa, **92-94**, 119
Sutton Ridge, 52
Sylvilagus,
 floridanus, **30**, 118
 obscurus, **31**, 118
 transitionalis, 31
Synaptomys cooperi, **56-57**, 118

Tab Cat Creek, 86
Talpidae **16-18**, 117
Tamias striatus, **32-33**, 118
Tamiasciurus hudsonicus, **37-38**, 118
Tapoco, NC, 68
Thomas Ridge, 26
Thunderhead, 54
Toad, 8
Townsend, TN, 72
Toxaway River Gorge, NC, 102
Transmountain Road; *see* Newfound Gap Road
Tremont, 17, 51, 64, 70, 76, 78, 82

Turtle, 58, 71
 Box, 91
 Snapping, 58
Twentymile, 83, 86, 91
Twentymile Creek, 26, 51, 78

Urocyon cinereoargenteus, **71-72**, 119
Ursidae, **73-77**, 119
Ursus americanus, 73-77, 119

Vespertilionidae, **19-28**, 117-118
Vole
 Meadow, **53-54**
 Rock, 2, 3, **54-55**
 Southern Red-backed, **52-53**
 Woodland, **55-56**

Vulpes vulpes, **70-71**, 119

Walker Creek, 78
Walker Prong, 10, 12, 40, 52, 54, 64
Walnut Bottom, 39, 71, 78, 83, 85
Wapiti; *see* Elk, American
Waynesville, NC, 68
Wear Cove, 36, 91
Weasel 9, 33, 35, 80
 Least, **102**
 Long-tailed, 1, 46, **81-82**, 119
Welch Branch, 92
Whistle-pig; *see* Woodchuck
Whiteoak Sink, 21, 22, 23, 27
White-tailed Deer; *see* Deer, White-tailed
White Rock; *see* Mount Cammerer
Wildcat; *see* Bobcat
Wolf,
 Gray, 4, 65, **67-68**, 69, 119
 Red, 1, 65, **69-70**, 76, 94, 98, 119
Woodchuck, 1, 2, 32, **33-35**, 66, 69, 70, 71, 118
Woods Rabbit; *see* Cottontail, Appalachian

Zapodidae, **62-64**, 119
Zapus hudsonius, **62-63**, 119